AF487740

DANCING IN THE DARK

How To Get The Most Out Of Life When Everything Is Falling Apart

BY DON ROBERTS

To my wife Nanette – the only one I dream of.

Table of Contents

INTRODUCTION

There's Too Much Dark In There

"There's too much dark in there, Daddy!" She is just four years old, terrified, pleading with her father to let her stay with her parents in their room in the middle of the night. In the daytime, she is a confident, independent, happy little girl. But in the evening, when the shadows close in around her, fear begins its reign of terror. Her vivid imagination kicks into overdrive, and suddenly her playroom teems with the creatures of the night. Fleeing their grasp, she runs to her parent's bedroom, armed with a certainty that her father can keep her safe. As he comforts her, he encourages her to go back to her room; that there is nothing to be afraid of. Again, she cries, "But Daddy, there's too much dark in there!" He replies, "Honey, there's just as much dark in here," to which she shoots back, "Yes, but it's a **better** dark in here!"

Are there times when there is "Too much dark" in your life? Are there things that frighten you and seem to close in on you in the tough times? If so, you're not alone! Life can get pretty scary at times. As we grow older, we get better at hiding our fears of the dark, but they are there just the same. If you've grown weary being afraid of your life, this book is for you. If you are tired of being hounded by things that seem to grip you and won't let you go, read on. Together, we'll discover that it's always a better dark when your Heavenly Father's there with you! He is a strong protector, who promises to be with you through the longest nights.

Dark times are a part of life. No one is immune – we all go through things that seem to snuff the light out of our lives. These seasons are unavoidable, painful, and overwhelming. As I write this, the dark cloud of the COVID-19 pandemic has descended on the globe. Depending on whom you believe, the numbers of people infected are staggering. The world has shut down, economies have tanked, and people are isolated with varying degrees of shelter-in-place orders. Business and Church leaders are tasked with learning how to operate in a changing landscape that no one in our lifetime has experienced before. The information seems to change daily, if not by the hour, requiring constant change in the face of this threat. Fear, anxiety, and frustration are at all-time highs, and no one seems to agree on what the best solutions are. No one is immune from this dark time, and no one is sure how long this will all last. It seems as soon as one obstacle is overcome, another rises to take its place.

But these times in the shadows can be some of the most productive seasons of our lives. Just as the little girl recognized, the dark is much more manageable when our Father is with us. There is something about these dreadful seasons that make us aware of our need for Him. The truth is, we are always needy, but we seem to be more aware of it while floundering in the quicksand of circumstances beyond our control. When we are overwhelmed, we turn to the only One who can rescue us. And when we do, He comes to us, though we don't always recognize Him in the midst of the crisis.

There are heartwarming stories coming out of this pandemic. Stories of heroic doctors and nurses, front line people in the service industries, selfless acts of sacrifice that encourage us all to seize the opportunities that dark times bring. Like mining for precious ore, deep beneath the surface of the earth, there are untold riches to be found in the darkest of times. Reaping those treasures are not easy, often requiring effort that is beyond us in normal times. In such seasons, we often reach our breaking points. I remember one interview with a nurse in New York at the height of their epidemic. She was coming off another twelve-hour shift in a week of long hours tending to the sick and dying. Overcome with emotion, the tears flowed freely as she pleaded with people to understand what they were going through. She talked about their own vulnerabilities to this disease, stating that just because they were medical professionals, they were not immune to infection themselves. She related the distance she had to keep from her own children and family members to avoid transmitting the disease to them. She had reached her breaking point, and who could blame her? Even the strongest amongst us will come to the end of ourselves in the dark times of life. No one gets a pass - life has both good and bad times - but Jesus promises to be with us through them all!

One of Jesus' most devoted followers, Mary, experienced dark times herself. There she was, head down, headed to the garden during the saddest time of her life. Jesus, the one who had rescued her from a life of misery and shame, was dead. Her champion was vanquished, and she was alone again. She was coming to finish the job of laying to rest the only one who had believed in her. Though it was now morning, it couldn't be any darker if it was midnight. And to make matters worse, when she arrived at the tomb, someone had stolen His body – or so she thought! That's the way it is during dark times. When you think you can't handle another setback, something else comes along that just overwhelms you. You see, in the dark, **everything** looks murky. Even the familiar, the safe, the comforting, can take on daunting proportions. You begin to live in worst-case scenarios-where your deepest fears seem to be coming true. Even the most optimistic souls can find their confidence wavering and their perspective fading in the darkness. So it was for Mary. In her discouragement, she couldn't see that Jesus was right there, waiting for her to look up! Finally, he prompts her with a tender question:

"Why are you crying? Who are you looking for?" (John 20:15 NLT)

In her grief, she didn't recognize Him! She thought He was the gardener, and in desperation asks if He took the body! Don't miss His answer - it's important. He could have scolded her for not seeing Him more clearly. He could have ridiculed her lack of faith. After all, hadn't he **told** them He would rise from the dead on the third day? Wasn't this the third day? But He doesn't do any of that. He just calls her name. "Mary." And notice her response. Immediately, she recognizes Him. Why? Because no one, no one had ever said her name like He did. He was the first to use her name with respect, with tenderness, with a purity of love she had never known. Before she met Jesus, Mary experienced some really tough times. She made poor choices out of a place of desperation. She was much more accustomed to men speaking her name with sinister intentions. Hers was a tainted reputation, giving some people license to shower her with disrespect and shame. But Jesus had changed all of that. When she met Him, she experienced something very different each time He used her name. When He called out to her, it was always with respect and honor, even when it was undeserved. Jesus had showed her the way out of the darkness, and in so doing He had forever changed her view of herself. As a result, His voice became memorable. She could pick it out of a sea of other voices. Jesus had promised that those that belong to Him would always hear Him well enough to follow Him:

My sheep recognize my voice. I know them, and they follow me.
(John 10:27 MSG)

A simple calling of her name from Jesus, and a burst of light flooded her soul, banishing the dark and filling her with hope. That's what your Father can do with dark times. He can turn the night into day, and draw you closer to Him than you ever dreamed possible. He really can make it a "better dark in there!"

That short conversation transformed Mary. Gone was her confusion and discouragement. She was now convinced – Jesus was alive, risen from the dead, just like He said! That news was just too good to be contained – she had to share it with everyone she cared about. She rushed back to find her friends, breathlessly proclaiming, "The tomb is empty – He is not there!"

Mary Magdalene went, telling the news to the disciples: "I saw the Master!" And she told them everything he said to her. (John 20:18 MSG)

Her friends didn't believe her at first. They were still shrouded in the dim confines of discouragement. It wasn't until they met Jesus personally that they were completely convinced. It's the same with you and me. We can be encouraged by other people's stories, but once we meet Him face to face, we will find a dance partner that we know we can count on.

CHAPTER ONE

It Takes Two To Tango

God's goal for you is not just to survive the dark times, He wants you to thrive during them. Instead of stumbling blindly through, He wants to teach you to Dance in the Dark! Most of us can dance through the good times of life, but when we face overwhelming circumstances, we need a dance partner. We need someone to lead us, someone who has been through this before, someone who knows where we need to go, and knows how all this will turn out.

On the popular television show, "Dancing with the Stars," celebrities are paired with professional dancers in a competition that plays out over several weeks. The task of these professionals is to first assess the abilities of the non-dancers, and then to help them make improvement every week. To become champions, they must master many different dances, each with their own challenges. The success of the celebrities is dependent not only on their willingness to work hard, but on how well they follow their professional's direction. They must trust their teacher to define their strengths and weaknesses, helping them to overcome their own deficiencies. The more skilled and experienced the professional is, the better it goes for the celebrity. But no matter how skilled their partner is, the star has to be willing to learn, willing to humble themselves and follow the direction they are being given. The champions always end up heaping praise on their dance partner, speaking in glowing terms of how much they helped them to become the best dancer they could be.

In the same way, we need a particularly skilled partner, one who can lead us through the most difficult seasons of our lives. This job is so daunting, so difficult, that the only one truly qualified is Jesus Christ! Look at how the writer of Hebrews describes Him:

"This High Priest of ours understands our weaknesses, for he faced all of the same temptations we do, yet he did not sin." (Hebrews 4:15 NLT)

He knows what scares us in the dark, He knows what causes us to freeze when we should be moving, because He has had to face those same fears Himself. He overcame them, and He knows how we can too! Look at His own words in John 16:33:

"I've told you all this so that trusting me, you will be unshakable and assured, deeply at peace. In this godless world you will continue to experience difficulties. But take heart! I've conquered the world." (John 16:33 MSG)

Jesus is not sugar coating the dark times–He tells us that we will have hard things to go through, but we don't have to back down when we do. He has already overcome everything that is trying to overwhelm us, so we can loosen up and dance right through those times knowing He is right there with us. He has said over and over,

"Never will I leave you; never will I forsake you." (Hebrews 13:5 NIV)

Because of this promise, we can be confident, because He is our dance partner:

"So we say with confidence, 'The Lord is my helper; I will not be afraid. What can man do to me?'" (Hebrews 13:6 NIV)

Too many times we are tied to the wrong dance partner! We let discouragement lead, but we end up even more depressed. We let bitterness take over our hearts, and start seeing the world through a victim's lens. Everything seems unjust, everyone else seems to get the breaks while we wallow in the muck of someone else's making. We let fear guide us, which causes us to use our God-given imaginations in perverse ways, always expecting the worst. When you think about it, both fear and faith require the same skill set: you must picture what hasn't yet happened as if it already has. As the writer of Hebrews says:

Faith assures us of things we expect and convinces us of the existence of things we cannot see. (Hebrews 11:1 GW)

Fear has the same ability! It assures us that things are bad and they are going to get worse. How many times have we worried about things that never came to pass? But while we were worrying, we were convinced that the thing we dreaded was really going to happen. And even if it did, the fact that we were worried about it did us no good! Jesus told us how foolish it is to let fear and worry take the lead in our lives:

Can all your worries add a single moment to your life? And if worry can't accomplish a little thing like that, what's the use of worrying over bigger things? (Luke 12:25-26 NLT)

Think about it, and ask yourself a question: How many things have you worried about that never ended up happening? For me, it's at least 90% - and in the 10% of times that did come true, worrying about it did not prepare me for the experience at all! If anything, I was more anxious as a result of sleepless nights spent fretting over what might happen. This rendered me less prepared to confront the challenge head on when it finally became a reality.

A couple of years ago, my wife Nanette suffered a massive heart attack while we were visiting our daughter's family in Washington State. I was awakened in the middle of the night by my daughter telling me, "Dad, I don't want you to worry, but the paramedics are downstairs with Mom, she's not doing well…" As I rushed to get dressed, my mind in a fog, I wondered if I had heard correctly. It was the Thanksgiving weekend, we were having a great time visiting, and had no idea when we went to sleep that night that we would be encountering the storm of our lives. Immediately my mind went into overdrive, trying to grasp the enormity of what we were facing. Would she survive? What if she doesn't make it? How will I lead the kids through this? How can I possibly go on without her?

My wife and I met and fell in love in junior high, when we were 13 years old. We've been "an item" ever since, so I literally don't know how to do life without her. She is my best friend, the one I KNOW that I can count on, the one that makes this life so much fun and so worth living. In that moment in time, I couldn't imagine a life with her not in the picture.

As the paramedics tended to her, I found myself numb and incapacitated emotionally. It was like an out of body experience. While I was present with them physically, my mind was churning away elsewhere, trying to make sense of it all. Dimly I heard one of the paramedics confirm that, yes, she was having a heart attack and needed to be rushed to the hospital. I was invited to ride along, and as they were getting her settled in the back of the ambulance, I sat there alone in the cab of the vehicle with my forehead pressed against the dashboard. My imagination was racing, visualizing a life without this sweet woman, and it was as if she had already died. As I was overcome with the deepest sadness I had ever experienced, I heard a still, small voice whisper to my heart, "I've got this. I've got her and I've got you and your family. Don, listen to me, all those years you have spent seeking my face in the early hours of the morning are going to pay off for you now. I will be with you and I will be with her and the kids. Trust me now, I'm here, you know my voice, press into me, I'll lead you through this."

I can't really explain what happened in the cab of that ambulance, but a peace descended on me in that moment, and somehow, I knew we would be ok. Interestingly enough, God had not assured me that Nanette would live through this experience, only that He had this under control and was with us as we went through it all. Time seemed to slow down for me, even as we were racing through the streets toward the hospital. The paramedic made small talk with me, and pointed out that if you had to have a heart attack, this was the right time and place for it! Seattle traffic can be brutal most times of the day, but at this wee hour on a Saturday Night/Sunday morning, we had the roads almost to ourselves. As we arrived at the hospital, they rushed my wife into a room with a team of surgeons and nurses who were awaiting our arrival. It was like watching a choreographed dance, each one with their role to play in ministering to my sweet Nanette. Once they prepped her for surgery, they rushed her back to the operating room, inviting me to run along behind them until they were just outside the surgical suite. We had been taking a shortcut through a brand-new area of the hospital, a critical care unit that was set to open to patients in the next few days. One of the nurses gently pushed me into an unoccupied room and said, "Stay here, someone will come and get you to take you to the waiting room…" and with that she ran off to catch up with the team ready to help my wife.

It was early, around 2 a.m. as I recall, and suddenly I'm left alone with my thoughts. It was weird being by myself in that wing of the hospital, with everything ready for patients but eerily empty except for me. I spent the next several hours there in the dark, all alone and seemingly forgotten by everyone except the Lord. I can't imagine what that time would have been like if I had not heard from Jesus in the ambulance. As it was, I knew I had to let the rest of the family know what had happened, as well as our friends back at our church in Sacramento, asking them to pray. I wasn't sure who to call first, and how to let people know how they could help us. When you've been a pastor as long as I have, you have plenty of experience being on the helping end for families in crisis. But it is a whole different experience being on the other side of things. In that moment, I didn't want to have to help others through their own shock and sadness at what was happening. I needed to reach out to someone who would take that role from me and just meet my needs and the needs of my kids.

Again, I felt the presence of the Lord bringing comfort to me, and reached out first to my brother Karl who lives in the Seattle area. He travels a lot for business, so I wasn't even sure if he was at home or on the road. I was calling in the middle of the night, and was aware that he might not even pick up, but to my relief, he did. As I explained what was happening, he said, "I'll be there in about 20 minutes, do you need anything?" My response? "A coffee would be great right now; this Californian is freezing in this hospital room!" He told me he would drive through Starbucks on the way, and tears came to my eyes! Such a small thing, but that simple offer to be with me and to bring me a coffee was as good as all the treasure in the world.

Part of the way Jesus makes good on His promise to never leave us or forsake us is to use people in our lives to be with us, especially in times of crisis. My brother came right away and spent the next couple of days right there in the hospital with my family and me, and it meant the world to me. Sometimes we think we have to do heroic things to make a difference in the world, but believe me, it's the small things that matter most when you are in the darkest of places. I will never forget the support my brother gave me when I was at my lowest point in life.

My daughter, Jourdain, was amazing through all of this as well. Though reeling herself, processing the same potential loss as I was, she became a steadying force to us all. She became a veritable "Nurse Nightingale," tending to our every need. Her husband Joel and our grandson Liam were with us through it all, including what turned out to be an extended visit with them after my wife was discharged from the hospital. Nanette was not allowed to fly for a couple of weeks, so we ended up staying with them in their home. Their welcome and service to us during that time was a healing balm to my wife and me. Liam, 5 years old at the time, made perhaps the biggest impact of all, when he crawled up into the recliner with Nanette, looked her right in the eyes and told her, "Mimi, you're my BEST friend…" That was a medicine far more effective than the doctors could ever have given her!

Looking back on that incredibly scary time, I am so grateful that Jesus showed up and offered to lead our own personal dance in the dark. Without Him, I would have let worry and anxiety lead, and would have ended up far more exhausted and worn out as a result. The truth is, Jesus is a much better dance partner. I highly recommend you accept His invitation the next time you are stuck in the dark. Believe me, you will hear Him say, "May I have this dance?" when you are overwhelmed by circumstances that you know are bigger than you are. No matter how weak you may feel, or how unskilled you feel you are when it comes to facing the dark, He can teach you to glide over the most scarred dance floors of life. But you might ask, "Will He have me?" The answer is an unqualified "YES!" In fact, He has already chosen you, and is just waiting for you to accept His invitation.

"You didn't choose me, remember; I chose you, and put you in the world to bear fruit, fruit that won't spoil." (John 15:16 MSG)

If you choose Him back, He will cause you to dance for joy, even in the most difficult circumstances. He's been doing this for His people for thousands of years. In the Old Testament book of Jeremiah, there is a wonderful picture of what He intends to do for you in the days ahead:

I will rebuild you, my virgin Israel. You will again be happy and dance merrily with tambourines. The young women will dance for joy, and the men—old and young—will join in the celebration. I will turn their mourning into joy. I will comfort them and exchange their sorrow for rejoicing. (Jeremiah 31:4,13 NLT)

So be encouraged, my friend. Jesus is a great dance partner. He will lead you through the most difficult of seasons, and you'll come out better for it. Each time He dances you through the battlefields, you will be more sure of His love and His ability to turn things around for you.

CHAPTER TWO

Dancing In The Dark

Glimpsed through teary eyes, I could see that she only had eyes for Him. As she gazed into His face, a look of wonder and girlish joy lit her countenance. He swept her across the dance floor in a graceful waltz that they both clearly enjoyed. No longer hampered by her disease-riddled body, she practically floated in His arms. They moved as one across a crystal sea, shining and basking in His radiance. The most beautiful light seemed to be coming directly from Him, and it lit the floor with an explosion of color. As I looked closer, I could see that the dance floor was in fact a huge bridge over a dark expanse. Beneath the riot of color was a vast chasm, which somehow, I knew was the gap between this life and eternity. Below was fearful darkness of the unknown. Above there was only the dance, insulating them from worry or stress. They seemed to have all the time in the world, as if time itself had been suspended. In no hurry to cross over, the joy on their faces mutual, they danced without a care in the world. I was struck by the amazing transformation that had taken place in her.

Moments before, my mother had been with us on her deathbed, her labored breaths coming farther and farther apart. Her poor body had wasted away to a mere 87 pounds, devoid of its strength and vigor. We were all there with her, my father and my siblings, along with our spouses and children, gathered to be with her in her last moments on earth. Now she was dancing, spinning safely in the arms of the One who always keeps His promises.

Mom was big on promises. As her health declined, she clung steadfastly to all that the Bible had to say about the dark times of life. She had practically wallpapered their home with post-it notes, covered with scriptures in her distinctive handwriting. "And we know that all things work together for good to them that love God, to them that are called according to His purpose." *(Rom 8:28)* would be plastered over the television set. "I am the Lord that heals you" *(Ex 15:26)* would be on the mirror above the bathroom sink. There were hundreds of them, stuck to the walls and furniture. We knew she was serious to put them everywhere like that. She had been an almost fanatical housekeeper, so to have that much clutter override her sense of order proved to us that she meant business.

She had been a believer for most of her life, and was a rock we all leaned on. Her faith was a comfort when we would go through tough times. You could be sure Mom was praying for you, not just saying she was. Nothing seemed to shake her, she was so SURE God would make a way through any difficulty we might face. She would listen patiently when I would pour out my frustrations, and would always point me back to the faithfulness of God and the certainty of His plan for us. Her faith had been forged through a lifetime of challenges. Raising seven kids on a limited income will do that for you. She and Dad never had it easy, but they inspired us with their love and commitment to each other and to us. With each setback, she would push forward, certain that better days were ahead.

So it was a bit unsettling during her final week on earth when she began to ask hard questions of her God. "Why is this happening to me?" she would ask. "I know your promises are true, so why have you not healed me?" Most troubling of all, she began to ask if ANY of it was real. "What if there is no heaven or hell? What if God doesn't really exist?" Our roles reversed; she was now asking me the hard questions.

Maybe you've done that in the darkness. Your faith seemed unshakable until THIS happened. Where you once found comfort, now you have only unanswered queries. If so, you're not alone. It's natural to ask, even necessary. God encourages it:

"Come now, let us reason together," says the LORD. (Isaiah 1:18 NIV)

He can take it. He has the answers. And He wants you to ask. Your faith will grow deeper, but asking questions can be troubling territory. It's not easy challenging deeply held, longtime beliefs. But if you will risk it, He will be faithful. As Mom discovered, He ALWAYS keeps His promises!

As I considered what my response should be to Mom's questions, it was if God was saying: "It's all right. I'm in this. Encourage her to ask me. I won't disappoint. I am here." So that's what I told her. "Go ahead, Mom, ask away. I don't know the answers, but He does." And so she did. Day by day, methodically reviewing the tenants of her faith, she talked to her God. I don't know what He told her, but can I say that week transformed her. As her body declined, her faith deepened, grew stronger. Always one to encourage, she became powerful in her statements to us. Throughout that long "death week," whether night or day, she would call to us one by one and tell us what the Lord had given her for us. Her encouragements and instructions were personal and specific. It was almost like a matriarchal blessing, that lifted and inspired. Let me give you one example:

It was the middle of the night. My siblings and I were taking shifts, watching over her, as the hospice nurses had told us she could go at any time. It happened to be my turn to keep watch over her that early morning, when I heard Mom whisper in the darkness, "go get your dad, I have something to say to him." I went and woke him up, telling him she was asking for him. He rushed to her side, and a few of us gathered around to hear her say to him, "kiss me." He tenderly bent down and gave her a peck on the lips. She said, "no, I want you to really KISS me." He did, while we all stared at the ceiling, the walls, any place but at them. When he finished, she looked him straight in the eyes and said, "Well done, good and faithful servant. You have kept your promise to me that you made on our wedding day. You have loved me as Christ loves His church. You have loved my kids as your own, (ours is a blended family) and you have been faithful to me. I want you to feel released when I go to be with the Lord, and if He brings someone to you to share your life with, you have my blessing." Dad, of course, protested, but she quieted him with a bit of humor: "I didn't say to go out **looking** for someone, only that it is alright with me if God gives you someone.

Besides, Honey, you're not meant to be alone." It was a tender moment, a holy moment. It was such a generous thing to do, it had to come straight from the heart of our giving God. The certainty in her was faith building for me. The closer she got to death, the surer she was that Jesus was waiting for her.

In the last few days, she would slip in and out of a coma. When she would wake up, she would be completely lucid, and would have something worthwhile to say that would encourage us all. She even kept her sense of humor. One time she woke up, said, "I feel like that cheesy commercial–but wait, that's not all, if you buy right now, we'll include this gadget with your order completely free of charge!" Each time she went to sleep, she expected to wake up in heaven. The first time that happened, she asked me, "Why do you think I haven't gone home yet?" I said, "I guess there's more for you to do yet." Settled, she said, "I guess He knows what time I'm supposed to go, doesn't He?" And He did. When all was ready for their dance, she was gone. And we were left with more confidence than ever that He really does keep His promises! Don't misunderstand me, I still miss her like crazy. But because of the way she danced with Jesus, I know that one day we, too, will take that dance with Him into Eternity. In the meantime, He promises to take our hand and dance us right through the dark times of this life.

CHAPTER THREE

Dead Man Dancing

"Dead Man Walking." A gruesome picture in just three words. Spoken to announce the last walk of a condemned prisoner, from a holding cell to the execution chamber. They are describing a person whose fate has been sealed - all appeals exhausted, with no hope of reprieve. Nothing left but to carry out the sentence. A tragic picture of a wasted life waiting to end. And in some ways, this sad phrase could describe each of us. We are prisoners of our own sin, condemned by our actions to die by a code of justice that simply cannot overlook what we've done. The Bible tells us that every one of us has a sin problem, that all of us have sinned and that sin must be paid for by death. To overlook that sin would be unjust and unfair to the ones hurt by our actions. Paul described our struggle this way:

I don't really understand myself, for I want to do what is right, but I don't do it. Instead, I do what I hate. But if I know that what I am doing is wrong, this shows that I agree that the law is good. So I am not the one doing wrong; it is sin living in me that does it. And I know that nothing good lives in me, that is, in my sinful nature. I want to do what is right, but I can't. I want to do what is good, but I don't. I don't want to do what is wrong, but I do it anyway. But if I do what I don't want to do, I am not really the one doing wrong; it is sin living in me that does it. (Romans 7:15-20 NLT)

Can you relate? How many times have you determined that today you will do better, today you will hold your temper, today you will be more patient with your kids, only to set a new personal low in human behavior? Let's face it, if you could have fixed this problem by now, you would have! It got so bad for Paul that he painted a particularly gruesome picture of his dilemma:

What a wretched man I am! Who will rescue me from this body of death? (Romans 7:24 NIV)

If Paul were writing to us today, he probably would have told us he had been tied to one of the Walking Dead! Imagine being tied face to face with a rotting corpse, the corpse of your victim. It's decaying body slowly corrupting your own, as you pay the price for your wrong doing. Staring into the lifeless eyes of that body of death, your mind would snap long before your body succumbed to the infection invading it from that corpse you can't free yourself from. Sin will do that to you – it corrupts every area of your life, there is no compartmentalizing this to one small area of behavior. It will stare you down, boring into your soul with a load of condemnation, guilt and regret. 'Guilty!' it proclaims over you as if it were judge and jury. It will convince you that you really are just a Dead Man Walking.

But I've got good news for you! When you are ready to face down your sin, Jesus comes face to face with you. He cuts you free from that body of death, and willingly takes its place as your dance partner. Now instead of death seeping into you, His uncorrupted nature flows into you, making you come alive for all eternity! He invites you to join Him in the dance of life, face to face, breathing life into you, just as He did when He first created Adam. (See Gen 2:7)

Jesus has done this for me more times than I can count. In my personal struggles to overcome my flaws and shortcomings, I've found that my efforts alone are simply inadequate to the task at hand. I'm a person who values discipline–I have learned how to stay fit physically, mentally and spiritually by exercising regularly. Because I've had success in these areas, my tendency is to attack every problem in the same way–to work harder and become even more disciplined in my behavior. The problem occurs when that is not enough. When I get to the end of myself, and no amount of discipline can shield me from my own selfish desires, I find myself discouraged and dejected.

I am competitive by nature. From my youngest days, I've enjoyed the process of trying to be the best. That worked well for me in the sports world, until I realized that there were other athletes that simply had more talent than I did. No amount of practice or effort was going to overcome that deficit. It was heartbreaking to realize that I was just not good enough to compete in the games that I loved. I didn't realize it, but a lot of my identity was wrapped up in being a baseball player, and the realization that I could not continue in that role was disorienting and discouraging. Somewhere in that process I met Jesus in a very real way. He began what has become a life long journey of discovery about who He has made me to be. Sometimes, when I get it right, I rise above my ingrained need to perform and be better than others. At other times, I fall into the trap of trying to prove my worth through comparisons, leaving me wanting in more ways than one. In such times, I tend to become judgmental and small, which is the exact opposite of God's will for my life. I end up feeling dry and lifeless, a shell of my true self. I begin focusing all my efforts on *looking* good rather than *being* good. If I can't succeed, I feel the need to at least look like I am! There is no way out of that trap without the Lord's help. Only when Jesus breathes new life into me do I find my real identity and only then can I begin to live the life He has destined me for.

There is a great picture of this in the Old Testament Book of Ezekiel. In Chapter 37 of that book, Ezekiel tells us of a time when the Lord took him to a dry valley filled with the bones of a vanquished army. God asks him the question; can these dry bones live? And to Zeek's amazement, they come together, perhaps to the old song, "The ankle bone's connected to the shin bone, the shin bone's connected to the knee bone…" Whole skeletons come together, then muscle and skin is added, until an entire fighting force is standing before him! But there is one problem. They still have no life in them. They aren't even the dead men walking, they are simply statues full of promise but with no life.

Maybe that is how you feel today. Your life looks good on the outside, perhaps, but you feel lifeless on the inside. You've lost your passion and it's all you can do to go through the motions of life. Can I tell you, friend, God has so much more for you than that! He wants more for you than the appearance of life, He wants to breathe into you so you are full of His life and inspiration.

___

Ezekiel's story didn't end with lifeless bodies standing in the desert. He is told to speak life over them, to ask for the breath of life to come into these dead bodies and that is exactly what happens! They became a great army again, ready to fight for each other and for all that God had promised them. What He promised His people long ago He promises you today: Life, and that more abundantly! *(John 10:10)*

He changes your destiny from "Dead Man Walking" to "Dead Man Dancing!" Or perhaps more accurately, "Formerly Dead Man Dancing!" With Jesus taking the lead, you can confidently face anything that may come your way. But fair warning: If you let Him lead in this dance, He will dance you right into the battlefields of life! Turn the page and we'll take a look at what that means for you…

CHAPTER FOUR

Dancing Through
The Battlefields

If you're going to dance with Jesus, you will find yourself dancing through battlefields. Here's why I say that: Jesus wants to dance with you, but He will always take the lead. If you've ever seen two people trying to dance together when both are wanting to lead, you know how ridiculous they end up looking. Instead of the grace of the waltz, they look like a couple of sumo wrestlers mauling each other across the dance floor! Jesus knows that you can't both lead, and He insists on that role. He does this not out of a desire to dominate you, but out of a conviction that He alone knows the very best use of your life.

Picture a ballroom dance floor with couples whirling around on the floor. The one leading can see where to go next, while their partner has to have great trust that they will not end up crashing into walls or other dancers. In the same way, you will spend a lot of your time dancing with Jesus without knowing what's coming. He has His eyes on everything, but you will have your back to a lot of the danger, often being blissfully ignorant of the threats all around you as He deftly guides you around them.

If you insist on leading the dance of life, you will end up crashing and burning, simply because you don't know where all the mines are buried! Jesus does, but He will respect your right to decline to follow His lead. If you choose to take over, you will find Him ever so politely shaking His head, letting you know He'll be right there for you when you decide to let Him lead again. He won't be party to your destruction, but He WILL be there to help you pick up the pieces! He will heal you and assure you that you can begin again, this time with Him in the lead.

Sometimes you want to lead because you want to avoid the risks of dancing through battlefields. In this mindset, you will end up living a too-small life. It's been said that such people live their lives as if the objective was to arrive safely at death's door. But Jesus has so much more for you than that! He calls you the light of the world, and gives you no less of an opportunity than to bring people He loves into right relationship with Himself. You are destined by Him to impact eternity, but you can't do that by playing it safe. To make a difference in the lives of people, you've got to get in the game… you were made for more than just cheering on a few superstar saints.

When my son Josiah was very young, I took him to his first major league baseball game. We chartered a bus for him and the other kids in our children's church and made the two-hour trek to the old Kingdome in Seattle to watch the Mariners play. Josiah was decked out in full uniform, glove in hand, chattering away excitedly as we motored up to the stadium. The excitement built as we climbed the stairs to the upper reaches of that concrete dome, and as we found our seats, his eyes were shining with excitement as he gazed upon that magnificent playing surface far below us. The first words out of his mouth were: "Ok dad, let's go play!" When I explained to him that we were there, not to play baseball, but to cheer on the most talented players in the league (Mind you, this was back when they fielded a championship-caliber team a LONG time ago) he looked at me like I had grown a second head on my shoulders. He simply could not believe that he was looking at the coolest playground he had ever seen and was expected to watch others have all the fun playing on it. No amount of popcorn, peanuts or crackerjacks could soothe his disappointed soul. After the game ended, I looked down at the poor disappointed boy and asked: "Were you a little bored here today?" He shot back: "I wasn't a Yitta bored, I was a Yatta bored!" In that moment, as I was laughing with him, it was as if I heard the Lord say: "Listen to your son! This is too often what my church looks like: a few talented players being watched and cheered on by all the rest of my people. I didn't create them to sit and watch others play, I want them to get in the game!" I've never forgotten that exchange. I know Jesus wants more for us, and when we let Him lead, we will discover that truth first hand.

But know this, Jesus will dance you through a life filled with challenge and danger. There is no avoiding this, because, there are unseen dangers all around you. You and I are in a battle every day, one that is often invisible to the naked eye but no less real than the great conflicts that are occurring in our world today. Look at Ephesians 6:12 with me:

For we are not fighting against flesh-and-blood enemies, but against evil rulers and authorities of the unseen world, against mighty powers in this dark world, and against evil spirits in the heavenly places. (Ephesians 6:12 NLT)

Yes, the world is far more dangerous than it appears! You have an enemy that is bent on your destruction. But take heart, you have a warrior leading you through the battle, and that truth can fill you with confidence and hope. That is why Jesus tells us to put our faith in Him:

"I told you these things so that you can have peace in me. In this world you will have trouble, but be brave! I have defeated the world." (John 16:33 NCV)

It is important to establish who's going to lead in your life. Remember, if you are leading, you are going to stumble because of troubles that are invisible to you. How many times have you said, "It seemed like a good idea at the time…" only to discover you had wandered into a minefield? To be fair, if Jesus is leading, you won't avoid the conflict either. He dances you through the battlefields knowing there are great victories to be won that can be only accomplished in times of crisis. The difference is, with Him in charge, you won't get taken out by the things you didn't see coming. You'll have His strength and resources to overcome such powerful opposition. He is ever vigilant, ever watchful, and nothing escapes His notice.

Take a look at how Jesus described this to His friend and handpicked disciple, a man named Simon Peter:

I'm telling you the very truth now: When you were young you dressed

yourself and went wherever you wished, but when you get old you'll have to stretch out your hands while someone else dresses you and takes you where you don't want to go." He said this to hint at the kind of death by which Peter would glorify God. And then he commanded, "Follow me." Turning his head, Peter noticed the disciple Jesus loved following right behind. When Peter noticed him, he asked Jesus, "Master, what's going to happen to him?" Jesus said, "If I want him to live until I come again, what's that to you? You—follow me."
(John 21:18-22 MSG)

Peter seems to be saying, "Ok, if I've got to go places I don't want to go, I'll do it–but what about John? Will he have to experience pain too?" But Jesus tells him, "let me worry about John. You've got enough on your plate with what I've got planned for you, believe me!"

Isn't that the way it goes? You try to make sense of the painful events of life, and looking around, it seems no one else is enduring what you're going through. Or if they are, they seem to be having a much easier time of it. They seem to be better resourced, or better connected to those who can provide relief in such difficult times. These comparisons can lead to feeling that God has favorites, but you're just not one of them. But what if there is a bigger picture here? What if there is purpose to your pain? What if God is determined to use you to help others who are going through difficulties alone, without Him leading them through it? What if He wants to position you in their lives so you can point them to the One who can lead them through those tough times? In the next chapter, we'll look at one of my favorite passages in the Bible, describing a time when God sent a couple of guys named Paul and Silas into a prison to reach an isolated, hurting man.

CHAPTER FIVE

Dancing (Not Whistling) In The Dark

The searing, blinding pain threatened to consume him. It hurt to think, let alone breathe. His clothes clung to the wounds on his back, each small movement tearing open the skin again. He willed himself to be still, lest the blood begin to flow again. He'd lost far too much as it was without causing himself more grief. The beating had been terrible, even for a man accustomed to pain and suffering. Once again, his mind replayed the scene. The humiliation of being stripped in public, the terrible sadistic look of anticipation in his tormentors' eyes as the whip was raised. And then the pain. Unbelievable, overwhelming, searing pain. He desperately wanted to erase the scene from his memory, but it kept coming. As soon as the sorry affair would end, his mind would push play again. But just as the cycle began anew, he heard an incredible sound. He shook his head in spite of the hurt it caused. There was no mistaking that voice. Though weak and muffled as it flowed through cracked and swollen lips, it was there nonetheless. His old friend and mentor Paul was singing! Beaten as badly as he, still Silas heard the old man's praises. Somehow, he found himself joining in. Together they drew strength in praising the One who was worthy of all praise. They worshipped the God that was bigger than the hurt.

The other prisoners looked on dumbfounded. Their incredulous gazes locked on the two old warriors of the faith. Hearing them thank and glorify the one who had seemingly abandoned them was amazing. Who was this God who could command such adoring commitment? How could their God lift them above the despair and hurt so completely? And if he could do it for Paul and Silas, could he do it for them too?

The answer came in a thunderous crack. To their astonishment, the awful chains encircling their legs and arms fell to the ground. The prison doors flung themselves open as the earth beneath their feet shook violently. All eyes stayed steadfastly upon Paul and Silas, watching for a signal as to what to do next. No one doubted that God had shown himself to be larger than their circumstances.

Silas smiled knowingly. He knew everyone expected them to bolt and run. He also knew that they would stay exactly where they were. God had not allowed them to be imprisoned just to let them go. What would be the point in that? An act like that would be evidence that God was merely toying with them. No, his God was not like that. There was purpose in all that he did. Sometimes, the purpose would be clear to Silas. Sometimes it would not. But now more than ever, he was certain God was in control.

He saw the jailer rush in. He saw the confusion, heard the despair. It seemed ironic that the tables had turned so completely. The once proud, evil tormentor was reduced to a scared and broken man. Knowing the penalty for allowing prisoners to escape was slow and painful death, it was not surprising the man should consider suicide. But in spite of the pain this man had caused him, he was in complete agreement with Paul when he shouted "Don't harm yourself, we are all here!" He watched the jailer fall to his knees and ask: "What must I do to be saved?" Suddenly Silas knew God's purpose for the whole affair. This wretched, miserable creature was loved by God and not forgotten by Him. Outcast and rejected by everyone, God had seen his pain. He would never have come to God on his own, so God was coming to him. Silas understood what God had known beforehand - this captor's pain was far deeper than the physical suffering he and Paul were experiencing. He found himself grateful, truly grateful to be counted worthy to suffer for the Lord's name's sake. His wounds were real, but they would heal. He rejoiced that now, because of God's great compassion, the jailer would heal too.

As the years passed, Silas would be reminded of this event time and again. As the cold weather would aggravate his old wounds, he would remember God's grace. He carried his scars gladly, knowing he would never forget the depth of God's love.

There is a generosity that rises from within us when we understand that God never wastes a painful time. We begin to experience what Silas did in this story, a desire to see others benefit from our pain. One of the most vivid examples of this in my life has been watching my good friend Sarah go through a time of tremendous loss. She was on a cruise in the Caribbean, enjoying a well-earned break with her husband and kids. Life was good, the church they had started together had become a thriving community, and Sarah's real estate business was booming. Their four young kids were happy, and the future never looked brighter. All that came crashing down around them when Sarah's husband Sheldon died suddenly after a rousing game of basketball on board the ship. No one saw this tragedy coming, least of all Sarah. She was going through the storm of storms, and I have never seen anyone handle pain like she did. She was brutally honest about her experience, and yet she has been incredibly generous to all of us as she shares what she is learning though this tragic time. Sarah led the memorial service for Sheldon, and it was one of the most impactful experiences of my life. Already a gifted communicator, she went to a new level that day. She invited us into what she was experiencing in a way that all of us benefitted from the pain she was going through. She made us laugh and cry at the same time, and the overall impact was life rising out of the ashes of tragedy. It was a display of raw emotion and fierce faith that avoided all the clichés and drilled right down to the truth about life and death. Word got out quickly and the service was viewed by a huge audience online, lifting the hearts of friends and family as well as perfect strangers. Her posts in the two and half years since Sheldon's death have been life-giving in the extreme. She has not held back, sharing the highs and lows of her journey. I am looking forward to the book she will one day write about all of this, but in the meantime, if you want to be encouraged, follow her online at **Sarah Koch /** **www.facebook.com/sarahmkoch.**

The next time you find yourself in the dark, remember Sarah's and Silas' stories. Know that there are those who live in the dark, who desperately need to see the light. And remember that God just may have put you there so they could bask in the reflected light of His love through you.

Instead of whistling in the dark to try to calm your fears, try singing! There just may be a jailer nearby who needs to escape the prison of despair.

CHAPTER SIX

When Your Coat Is Gone

I wonder, was it dark in there? Alone in the pit, hearing your brothers discuss their plans to end your life, or at best to sell you into slavery. All that was bad enough. But to be without your treasured coat? The one that meant so much to you, because your dad had given it to you? The coat that reminded you every time you wore it how much he loved you. The symbol of his favor that never failed to bring a smile to your lips when you looked in the mirror. You were the special one, and everyone knew it. Sure, your family resented you, but that only added to the satisfaction of being Dad's favorite.

But now all that had changed. The coat was gone, stripped by those jealous siblings. You wonder: is Dad's love gone as well? You've heard their scheming, and know their plans. Cover their sin of selling you to the slavers by covering the coat in blood. Tell Dad the terrible news. "We found Joe's coat, Dad. We looked all over for him. He must be dead-couldn't have survived. Some wild animal must have torn him apart." Sure, your father will grieve, but he'll get over it. After all, he has a lot of other sons, and eventually you'll become only a distant memory.

It must have been dark in there. But as Joseph would discover, his Papa and God would never leave him. So it was a better dark for knowing that. Look at his life, follow the purpose. No matter how bad things got, his Heavenly Father was always there. And as a result, Joseph persevered and others benefited from his life.

See, God had big plans for Joseph. Unknown to anyone but God, a world famine was coming, and Joseph was the one God had chosen to do something about it. It was time to get Joseph ready for the huge responsibility of keeping the people of the world from starving. He would need patience. He would need discernment. He would need empathy, and he would need to get organized. And God was going to provide all of that for Joseph through some very dark times ahead.

His Father and Creator, who loved him even more than his earthly father did, had to dance him through a brutal training ground. There in the dark, the qualities Joseph would need most would emerge. In the pain of abandonment, in the crucible of discouragement, God would forge in him an unshakable confidence that would enable him to navigate the worst the world could throw at him.

As things went from bad to worse, Joseph learned that God would never leave him alone. He became convinced it would all work out, though the circumstances seemed to scream that the opposite was true. His brothers were going to kill him, but had a change of heart. As he waited in the pit, he could hear them arguing about his fate. One of them gets the bright idea, "Hey, let's sell him instead! There's no profit in killing him. We'll ship him off to some foreign traders, and Dad will be none the wiser! Show him the coat, dipped in sheep's blood, and he'll be convinced. Joseph will be out of our lives forever, and we'll make money in the meantime!"

Some brothers, huh? But maybe you know what Joseph was feeling – those who should have been a safe harbor were not. Someone you should have been able to trust with your life, took what was most precious to you. Your dignity and honor are in tatters, while your tormentors seem to go on untouched. Why would God do such a thing? If He loves you like everyone says, why didn't He protect you? Big questions-valid questions, with no easy answers. Perhaps there are more promises than answers right now, and that's ok.

I know I can relate, at least on some level. While my life has never been threatened, being in a leadership position for these four decades has opened me up to plenty of criticism. Now, without a doubt, much of that has been earned, owing to my flaws and shortcomings. But at other times, I have been amazed at the things people choose to believe about me that just can't be substantiated by facts. Their responses seem way out of proportion to the perceived offense. When that happens, it hurts; there is no getting around it. If you're like me, you end up wasting all kinds of emotional energy trying to figure out why they have turned on you. I end up having long conversations with offended people in my head, without giving them the benefit of responding for themselves. Instead, I put words in their mouths in response to my questions, and often my imagination fills in the worst possible answers to my scathingly adept accusations. This gets me nowhere closer to resolving the conflict, but rather is like pouring gasoline on the flames of my resentment at their harsh treatment of me. Instead, it brings out the worst in me, causing me to be suspicious of others who have not yet betrayed me. The whole thing can become a spiral into despair, unless I learn to let God shoulder the responsibility of judging other people's actions toward me. I am simply too limited to be able to understand why people do what they do, whether good or bad. I know that I am often the recipient of tremendous grace from people as they bless me far more than I deserve. It is truly humbling to hear that people are praying for me and asking God to give me favor and meet my needs. We don't know the backstory of people's lives, but God does. He knows because He can see into their hearts while we are left on the outside looking in. Take a look at this verse from the Old Testament:

The LORD does not look at the things man looks at. Man looks at the outward appearance, but the LORD looks at the heart." (1 Samuel 16:7b NIV)

Since God has the ability to see within people, He knows the reason behind every action, even when we don't know why we do what we do. Have you ever done something crazy, only to wonder what in the world got into you to make you do something like that? At such times, it is important to remember that God does know why and is uniquely qualified to help us work through both our sin and the hurts that others cause us by their judgments.

"...for the LORD searches every heart and understands every motive behind the thoughts..." (1 Chronicles 28:9b NIV)

Let's return to Joseph's story and learn from his experiences. He had years of trials and tribulations, and it took many more years to understand why those dark times were necessary. He will discover over time that God's provision many times looks like anything but. Watch for it as we continue our journey together through Joseph's life.

The brothers' plan is culminated when some slave traders happen by. The negotiations begin, and before you know it, Joseph is on his way to Egypt. He lands in the household of a man named Potiphar, who was a captain of the guard for Pharaoh, King of Egypt. Everything Joseph did, God blessed. Noticing this, Potiphar put him in charge of everything he owned. But Potiphar wasn't the only one who Joseph impressed. Potiphar's wife had very different plans for him, and begged him again and again to come to bed with her. Joseph refused, and his reward was to be falsely accused of raping the wife. This lands him in jail. As the injustices seem to be piling up for our friend Joseph, he could have given in. He could have looked out for himself. But he continues to choose the right path, doing the right thing, no matter the cost. Somehow, he knew that God was still with him, and there would be a greater purpose served in the end.

Look at the account in the book of Genesis:

"But the Lord was with Joseph in the prison and showed him His faithful love. And the Lord made Joseph a favorite with the prison warden." *(Genesis 39:21 NLT)*

Before long, the warden put Joseph in charge of running the prison, which ran more smoothly than ever. As his administrative skills increased, so did his compassion for his fellow prisoners. A couple of the King of Egypt's servants fell out of favor and into the prison where Joseph was. They each had dreams, and he saw that they were upset by them. He was learning to be sensitive that way, to pick up on other people's pain. Dark times can do that for you. Where you once might have been quick to judge, you now understand. Sometimes life dumps on you. No reason. Hard things come to us all, and there isn't always a good reason for it. It's in those dark times, when you can't see the light at the end of the tunnel, that compassion is born. Empathy is a powerful thing, but comes at a considerable cost. Joseph knew all too well what it was to live at the whim of those more powerful than he. And this would equip him uniquely in the future, when, to his amazement, he would become the second most powerful man in the known world, after Pharaoh himself.

Joseph encouraged the two servants to share their dreams with him, telling them that God will not leave them in the dark forever. Wonder where that conviction came from? His long years in the darkness were forging a conviction that, no matter what, God never abandons His kids. He is there every step of the way, through some of the most unimaginable experiences possible. No fair-weather friend, He would stick by you when no one else did. So they share their dreams, and Joseph generously interprets them—for the wine taster, it was great news. In three days, he would be lifted out of prison, restored to his old position of trust and respect. I wonder, was that hard to swallow for Joseph? His heart's desire, to finally be rid of the shame and the darkness, is promised to another. Would his time ever come? Would he ever see the end of all this pain and misery? Was life in the sunshine of God's favor in the cards for him at all? Or was he doomed to a lifetime of darkness, always helping others but never being helped himself? He must have asked these questions, but still he remained steady. You can hear the pain and the hope against hope in his request of the wine taster:

"And please remember me and do me a favor when things go well for you. Mention me to Pharaoh, so he might let me out of this place. For I was kidnapped from my homeland, the land of the Hebrews, and now I'm here in prison, but I did nothing to deserve it." (Genesis 40:14,15 NLT)

Unfortunately, though the wine taster promised to bring Joseph's request before the King, he promptly forgot all about him and went back to his old life. Two years pass by, and still Joseph is stuck in the dark. But finally, when all hope must have been gone, God lifts Joseph out of the prison. In one glorious day, he is transformed from lowly prisoner to second in command of all of Egypt. Apparently, Joseph was finally ready. He now had everything he would need to lead with compassion and with wisdom. The King, you see, had a dream as well, two in fact. No one could interpret the dreams for him, and finally the wine taster remembers Joseph. He tells the king of the man in prison who had a gift, an ability to interpret dreams. Immediately the king calls for Joseph to be brought before him. God granted Joseph the ability to know what these two dreams meant, and they were significant dreams. The entire world was about to experience seven years of incredible plenty, but then seven years of famine would follow. These hard years would be so bad, no one would remember the good times. If the king was wise, Joseph said, he would appoint someone to manage the plenteous years, so there would be enough for everyone during the famine that would follow. The King's response must have been incredible to Joseph's ears:

"'Can we find anyone else like this man so obviously filled with the spirit of God?' Then the King said to Joseph, 'Since God has revealed the meaning of the dreams to you, clearly no one else is as intelligent or wise as you are. You will be in charge of my court, and all my people will take orders from you. Only I, sitting on my throne, will have a rank higher than yours.'" (Genesis 41:39,40 NLT)

And just like that, as quickly as it had all gone bad, he was in charge of the greatest nation on earth at that time. It works that way sometimes, for no apparent reason, things get better. You don't know what you did to deserve the bad times, and you can't point to anything you did to cause the good times. And that's the point–we're not in control, God is! He knows how to get us ready; He knows what we will need, and He'll use the good and the bad to equip us. He has promised, after all:

"And we know that God causes everything to work together for the good of those who love God and are called according to his purpose for them." (Romans 8:28 NLT)

Joseph, now skilled in managing an important household & a lowly prison, would handle these new responsibilities with great wisdom and sensitivity to the needs of the people. He stored up much in the good times, and distributed it with care in the hard times. Because he never forgot what it was like to endure hardships, he could relate to those in need. He did not lord it over his charges during the years of famine, saying: "you should have planned better during the years of plenty like I did." Instead he reassured the people that they would get through this together, that he had stored up enough for them all. If Joseph had been given the task without the preparation of all those hard times, I wonder what kind of leader he would have been? If all he had ever known was life as a favorite son of a wealthy man, could he have managed to care for the hurting so well? I imagine he would have had a very difficult time relating to those who had never had it easy. He would have been ill-equipped to help the vast majority of people who he would be asked to lead during one of the most difficult times in human history. But God knew how to get Joseph ready for his life's work, and he knows how to prepare you as well. Joseph's life shines like a beacon to us in the darkness, assuring us that God will not waste this difficult time. He will be with us through it all, and he will give us an understanding of what others are going through.

I began my ministry career fairly early in life, becoming a youth pastor at the tender age of 19. I was barely older than the kids I was leading, and had no idea what I was doing. I was fairly new in my relationship with Jesus, but I knew I loved Him with all of my heart and I was learning to love the people that He had died for. A big part of my equipping came from my early years, being raised in a loving and stable home. God had seen fit to let me win the parent lottery–I benefitted from a dad and mom who truly loved my siblings and me. Though we didn't have much by way of material things, they consistently demonstrated selfless love for all of us. Both of them willingly made sacrifices for our well-being, of which we were often completely oblivious to. When finances dictated having cereal or pancakes for dinner, they made us think it was just because they wanted us to have a cheat meal, not burdening us with the knowledge that they couldn't afford groceries that week and were using up what was left in the cupboards. They were generous with their praise and made sure I knew that they loved me, and modeled what repentance looked like when they failed. All of this was great, and I have wonderful memories of my growing up years. Those experiences allowed me to love others as I had been loved. But there was an equipping that I was still lacking. Not everyone I was called to minister to had the same upbringing as me. In fact, some of them had experienced the polar opposite. They had plenty of material things, but were completely dysfunctional in giving and receiving love. Some of them had suffered neglect, others outright abuse. Without some real pain in my life, my answers to their very real questions would end up sounding simplistic and naive. God surely knew this would be the case, so He led me into my first real battlefield of pain.

My college roommate and I had been best friends since our childhood days. We always said we would go off to college together, and sure enough, when I graduated from high school, I followed him to San Jose State University in Northern California. He was a year older than me, and we agreed to room together, along with two other friends that we had met there at school. It was a season of firsts for me, my first time away from my parents' home, first time on an airplane, first person in my family to graduate high school let alone go to college. I had no idea what I was doing, but it was a comfort to have my best friend there to help guide me. He showed me the ropes, sharing last year's text books with me and helping me adapt to life on my own. It was during that first year away that God began to draw me near to Him personally.

We were a church going family growing up, and not attending weekend services was out of the question. We simply weren't given that option— we were going to be there with our parents every week, rain or shine. I went to honor my parent's wishes, but was often bored and church became something of an endurance contest. I didn't know God personally yet, I just went with my family to church; we thought that was what good Americans should do.

When I went away to college, for the first time in my life, I had a choice about going to church, and it was great to be able to sleep in on Sundays like "normal" people. But to my surprise, after a few weeks of that, I found myself wanting to go. I asked to attend church with my roommate's parents, since they were members of the same denomination as my family, and they were delighted to have me come along. In fact, they began bugging my roommate with dumb statements like, "why can't you be more like Don, and come to church with us…" Little did I know that this was creating a resentment in my friend that was simmering to a slow boil. Add that to my own immaturities and you have a recipe for disaster. A storm was brewing, though I had no idea what was coming…

During the long Christmas break of my second year, I received a letter from my roommate and best friend stating that he and the guys in our apartment no longer wanted to be roommates with me. He said they had already packed up my stuff and it would be waiting for me on the front porch when I wanted to come get it. I felt completely blindsided by this action, as I really had no idea we were at that big of an impasse in our friendship. With no previous pain to guide me, I felt abandoned and lost. I didn't have the resources to get my own apartment, and the school term was about to start the following week. I wanted to fight back, but I didn't know how. My name was on the apartment lease, so I knew they couldn't just kick me out, but I couldn't imagine trying to share a living space with guys who felt that hostile towards me. It left me with no option but to withdraw from school for the spring term and move back in with my parents. It was humiliating and hurtful. Always a hard worker, I applied at all kinds of places of employment, bent on saving up enough to get back to school in the fall. Every door remained closed to me, and I couldn't find a job to save my life. I felt completely stuck; running in place. But God was at work in my life. He had been drawing me closer to him during my time in college, and now was meeting me in my time of despair.

I began to listen to the Bible on tapes, which was a brand-new technology at the time. I busied myself beautifying my parent's landscape, and listened to the New Testament for hours a day. I started attending my parents' church, which was a whole new experience. They had left our old denominational church in favor of a small startup, and I went along again to honor my parents. It couldn't have been less relevant to me at the time, as it was extremely small and pastored by an Arkansas transplant who played country music way before country was cool by anybody's standards, besides my dad. He had a heavy southern drawl and seemed completely out of touch with me, as I was a long-haired rock and roll fan. The services seem backward and simple to me, and yet there was something going on beneath the service that was appealing to me. There was something real about those times, though I had no idea at the time it was the presence of the Holy Spirit. The pastor took me under his wing, and began to teach me what having a personal relationship with God was all about. We made an unlikely pair, but through his mentorship, I found my purpose in life. He taught me to love the Bible, to see in its pages the wisdom that applied to every one of life's situations.

That relationship with my pastor helped me to understand the purpose in the pain of my roommate's rejection. He showed me in the pages of the Bible many of the concepts we're exploring here in this book together. All of these years later, I am more convinced than ever that God never wastes painful experiences. It is in the context of relationships that we learn the most important lessons in life.

We are in this together. God has given us this life, filled with joy and pain, and asks us to work it out alongside one another. Others will experience pain that you have experienced. The last thing they need in those times of darkness is someone who has never been there before. Darkness marks us and makes us recognizable to others who travel those difficult roads. When fellow travelers share their pain with us, they know that we know when we share with them the lessons we've learned. You know what it is like to have someone try to encourage you when they have no idea what you're going through. But I'm sure you can recall someone who seemed to understand, who knew when to speak to you and to walk with you quietly. You, like Joseph, are destined to help others. You, too, will learn the faithfulness of the God who dances you through the darkness.

Before we leave Joseph's story, let me ask you a few questions: What about you? What does **your** coat look like? What is your symbol of God's love and favor? Is it your marriage? Perhaps your career? Or maybe your health? It may not be multicolored, but it's there nevertheless. The one thing that tells you He's there. Your proof to the world that you're His special child, obviously well-loved. Your heavenly Father has always given good gifts, but He never intended them to be the proof of His love. Why? Because gifts have a way of wearing out, or getting lost, or stolen, or destroyed. And when they're gone, what then? If they are proof of His love, then is His love absent when they are taken away? That's the danger in seeing God's blessings as validation of His love. They are fleeting, but His commitment to you is eternal.

Or maybe you're one of those who felt that you were on the outside looking in. Others always seemed to be the ones with the special coats. You were the one with the hand-me-downs. They prospered, you struggled. They got the promotion; you were passed over...again. Their marriage blossomed, yours failed. You tried to tell yourself it didn't matter, but it did. God seemed to have favorite kids, and you weren't one of them. When you heard the testimonies of blessings, you smiled on the outside but inwardly you cringed. Another reminder of your lack of status with God.

If you have felt that way, you are not alone. The truth is, most of us have been down that road a time or two. Very few have truly been included the "in" crowd. We were not the head cheerleader or captain of the football team. Many of us know what it is to be outcast, to be looked down upon. But as Joseph discovered, His heavenly Father was with him through it all. He was stripped of his coat, his family, his standing, but not of his God. And somewhere in the darkness, he realized that things don't matter very much. Things can be taken away from you, but God's love remains. In fact, it is in the darkness that we see His light shine the brightest. When all others fail, He will not. He is with you, whether anyone but you believe that or not!

CHAPTER SEVEN

You Made Your Bed, Now Sleep In It

"How did this happen to me?" He cried to himself. But he knew the answer. This was all his doing. Covered in mud and God knows what else, he finally came to his senses. There in the pig pen, miles and miles from the town in which he was so lovingly raised, he thought to himself: "**I** did this to me! What was I thinking? How could I waste all that my father gave to me? He raised me better than that! But I thought I knew better - what I wanted, what I needed. Now it's all gone, and I can't fix this. I'm tired of pretending. I'm going home. My father's servants are better off than me, and he has always been merciful. Maybe he'll let me come home, not as a son, I've thrown that privilege away. But I could serve him, I know I could!" So he set off for his childhood home, rehearsing his lines as he went. "I'm sorry, Dad, I really am. I know I've sinned against both you and God. I want to live here again, not in your house of course, but out with the servants. I don't deserve to ask this, but let me be your servant, I beg you!" Over and over he spoke the words, refining his plea for mercy. "It'll never work, he thought, but I've got nowhere else to turn! It just has to work!" But still the doubts crept in. "Dad will be so mad at me, and he should be. He worked hard all his life to leave me an inheritance, and I've squandered it all! And my brother, he'll blow a gasket! How well I remember the look of utter disgust he gave me as I traipsed off with my newfound wealth. He was right to look at me that way!" He almost turned around a dozen times. But desperation drove him on. "Maybe, just maybe, my father will find it in his heart to forgive me…"

He shook his head in disbelief. Sitting here now, in his father's house, the guest of honor, who would have believed it? The family ring on his finger, new clothes on his back to replace his filthy rags. His father sitting next to him, grinning from ear to ear. Everyone celebrating and life back to normal. No matter how he played it out in his head, he never could have imagined how it could have turned out this way. His mind drifted back to that incredible reception, just a few hours ago. Head down, running through his lines for the hundredth time, he crests the familiar rise in the road that signaled he was close to home. Looking up apprehensively, he rubs his eyes and shakes his head in wonder. Could it be? Could that be his father running towards him? He's still so far off, he could only have noticed me if he was looking for me. After all this time, has he really been watching for me? Before he knew it, his father had him in a bear hug, laughing and crying at the same time.

He started into his speech, "I'm so sorry, dad, I don't deserve to be called your son ever again..." But his father wasn't listening to him! Instead, he was shouting for the servants, "Quick, come quickly! My son is finally home! Let's have a party to celebrate the day you thought would never come! I told you God would bring him back! My son is home at last!" His joy was infectious, and suddenly he was surrounded by a cheering throng.

"How did this happen to me?" he thought to himself. "This is none of my own doing. I could never have expected this after all I have done. I threw it all away, and now it is being returned to me a hundred-fold! Such grace, so undeserved!"

Can you relate? See, not all darkness happens **to** us. Some of it, we bring on ourselves. That may be the toughest kind of all. When the injury is self-inflicted, we are tempted to prolong it, believing we deserve it after all we've done. If we are not careful, we may never emerge from the gloom of self-pity. The answer is not another pep talk. It's not about pulling ourselves up by our bootstraps and making something of ourselves. It begins in understanding just who our Heavenly Father is. That's why Jesus told us the story of the Prodigal Son, so we could see what God thinks about us when we've brought the shadow of condemnation down on our heads.

The story of the Prodigal is a parable, meaning Jesus is making it up. He carefully crafts a tale that teaches, one that sheds light on one of life's most common experiences. All of us blow it, we all do stupid things we wish we hadn't. We pull the wool of self-deception over our own eyes, and then have no idea how to come back into the light. But the father in his story is meant to show us the way out. He stands waiting, day after day, for as long as it takes, for us to come to our senses. He waits patiently for us to realize we simply cannot fix our problems. When we finally come to the end of ourselves, our heavenly Father is ready and willing to welcome us home. He is not smugly anticipating our self-humiliation, but rather eagerly waits to restore our dignity and our standing as one of His very own. When the darkness of our own poor choices closes in on us, He is waiting to bring us into the light. We can never lose our standing with Him, no matter how dumb our actions are! We will always be His son or daughter, and He wants us to live with confidence that His ways really are better than our own.

The Prodigal teaches us of another kind of darkness as well. That is the darkness of judgment. The wayward son had an older brother who never forgave his brother for taking off and leaving the family. While his father is rejoicing, he is seething. "Typical." He spits the word from his mouth. "This low life loser of a brother comes slinking home and what does dad do? Throws him a party, for crying out loud! When did he ever do that for me? I'm the faithful one, but do I get a celebration? No! I do all the work, and he gets all the reward. He deserves to be thrown out, not paraded about like he's done something great with his life!" He stalks off in disgust, sulking in ever deepening shadows of judgment. His watchful father notices he is gone, and typical of him, he goes looking for his son. "What's wrong, my son? This is a day of great celebration, why do you look so miserable?" "What's wrong?" his son shoots back, "Are you kidding me? I've never given you one moment of trouble all these years, and you barely notice. But this brother of mine throws it all away and you honor him like this? Where's the justice in that? Do I have to go out and make a mess of my life to get you to notice?" But the father patiently explains to his son, "the stuff is not the reward, my son. It is my presence. You have been with me all this time, and have basked in the light of my love. Your brother has lived in the shadows for far too long, and now he is finally back in the family. We are together, your brother, yourself, and me. And that is always a reason to celebrate!"

Our reward does not come in the form of the things God blesses us with. It is His irrevocable invitation to be in His family that will lead us into the light. Simply being with Him, knowing you are a valued member of His family is a treasure worth more than all the riches this world has to offer. So the next time you find yourself wallowing in a pigpen of your own design, don't stay there another minute. Get up and come home to the Father who is eagerly awaiting your return!

CHAPTER EIGHT

Things That Go Bump In The Dark

He would remember that sound for the rest of his life. The *whoosh* of air and the resounding *BOOM* of the great door slamming shut would stay with him forever. The strange silence that followed. And the utter, complete **darkness.** There was a finality to it, a quality you could *feel*.

Slowly other sounds began to register there in the dark. The fumbling of his family members trying to light the lamps. The restless movement of the animals unaccustomed to being enclosed. And then, faintly, the sounds that would feed his doubts and hurt his heart. Drifting through the thick walls was the sound of laughter. Not the joyful variety, but mocking, jeering, pain-inflicting laughter. You know the kind. The snickering of your coworkers after you've been passed over for that promotion *again*. The self-righteous tittering of your friends as they discuss your divorce. "I knew it would never last," you hear them say, and the phrase is burned indelibly into your mind.

He heard the insults. He'd heard them before. "Crazy old Noah. Spent his last dime building that boat. A *boat*, for crying out loud! Here in the middle of nowhere, *miles* from the nearest water. And now he's shut up in there with all those animals-for **what?**" There in the dark, that last "for what" pierced his soul. "What if they're right? What if the rains don't come?" For seven long days he pondered the questions in his mind. The rain that would flood the earth didn't start for seven days, *(See Gen 7:10)* so Noah had to endure those derisive comments all that time. He had to be wrestling with doubts about what he had heard God asking him to do. As the days stretched into a week, he had to be tormented with the second guessing that comes in the waiting times. My pastor once described such times as "the long middle." That time between the promise and its fulfillment can seem like an eternity. We grapple in the gap times, and often the questions outnumber the answers.

Darkness and delays will do that to you. Your confidence begins to erode away before the rushing river of doubt. Don't think you're alone when you have a crisis of confidence in the midst of difficulties. Jesus himself cried out on the cross, "My God, My God, why have you forsaken me?" Since Jesus never sinned, it must not be sin to utter questions while in the dark. But notice what He did with those fears - He cried out to God, knowing that it's always a better dark when you're with the Father. His Father answered Him by raising Him from the dead, and He'll answer you, too.

So ask away. He can take it. He wants to be with you in the difficult spaces–He's no fair-weather God. It's in the tough times that you find out who your friends are. Everybody likes a winner, so when you're on top, they're there. But when things turn sour, they run for cover. But not your Heavenly Father. He's promised to be with you, no matter what.

God has said, "I will never leave you; I will never forget you." So we can be sure when we say, "I will not be afraid, because the Lord is my helper…" (Hebrews 13:5b-6 NCV)

Knowing He's there with you is a fear killer. And that's important, because fear lives in the dark. You know what I mean. Fear cozies up to you when the light fades, and whispers slyly in your ear: "What if…" Your mind races with the possibilities. "What if this never gets better? What if rescue doesn't come?" But then you hear another whisper, this time a steadying, gentle voice. "It's all right. I'm here. I'll always be here." And somehow you just KNOW. Circumstances have not changed, but you have. No matter what, you know you're not in this alone. Hope begins to dawn, however dimly, in the dark. When it does, fan that flame! Put your hope in Him, because He really will keep His promise to you. You will not only survive this, you will THRIVE, because He is leading you through.

Even when I walk through the darkest valley, I will not be afraid, for you are close beside me. Your rod and your staff protect and comfort me. (Psalms 23:4 NLT)

I remember a dark time decades ago that a couple I knew went through. They were experiencing a particularly difficult time in their marriage. They were facing what looked like financial ruin, and their relationship was on the rocks. Harsh words had been thrown about, resulting in deep pain for them both. Things were escalating with each passing day. It was all going from bad to worse, when she found out she was pregnant. Now in good times, that might have been wonderful news. But at this time in their lives, it seemed to be more than they could ever handle. How could they bring a child into such trying circumstances? The marriage was probably going to end up dissolving, and neither of them felt they had the capacity to love a child in the midst of their pain. They honestly felt they were incapable of loving another human being in the state they found themselves in. They were damaged goods in their own eyes, and felt it would be a cruelty to bring a child into such circumstances. On top of all that, there was no money to raise a child. They were struggling to hang onto their business and their home. They couldn't possibly care for a new life in all of the chaos that had become their lives.

A decision was made to end the pregnancy and a date was set for the abortion. The news rocked all of us who loved them, as it was completely out of sync with their core beliefs. We all believed that life is sacred, and in our desperation, we pleaded with them not to go through with it. This dear couple was struggling so badly, they simply could not receive our support at that time. The pressure of this decision was the straw that broke the camel's back for their marriage, and they separated. Things were going from bad to worse, so we began to fast and pray, asking God to give them the strength to save this little one's life. As I prayed for them, I had the strongest sense of destiny on this unborn child's life. I was impressed that God was going to use this child to help many others. I was torn between hope and despair, but continued to add my prayers to the many others who loved this couple. The fateful day came, and the mother could see no other way out of her desperation, so she headed to the clinic tearfully determined to get this all behind her. But on the way, this first-time mom found a strength she didn't know she had. She realized she simply could not go through with it, and returned to her home. The marriage was over, there were no monies to support her and her child, and she was emotionally spent. But somehow in that moment she knew that God would be with her. And he was! She gave birth to a beautiful baby girl who has grown up into a wonderful mom and teacher of young children. Her life has had an incredibly positive impact on countless children over the years. So many families have been blessed by her selfless, loving service to their kids. Her life was almost ended before it began, but God intervened as only He can.

That experience changed me personally in many ways. I saw that God really does answer our prayers. I learned that He treasures each individual life and has a marvelous plan for us all. My faith grew through this near tragedy, and as a result I was better equipped to help others going through dark times in their lives.

Fast forward three decades. Dear friends of ours found themselves facing an unplanned pregnancy of their own. They were living wonderful lives and felt their family of three teenaged kids was complete. Their businesses were thriving, and they were happy together. But this news rocked them to their core. They simply could not see how, at this stage of their lives, they could parent another child. In their desperation, they asked to meet with my wife and I to discuss their options. They were under tremendous stress and as so often happens during such times, they could not seem to agree on what the best decision for them to make. It is common in such situations to turn on each other, venting fears and frustrations in less than healthy ways. But they trusted us to help them hear God clearly, and as often happens, my wife's words were the most helpful. Her assurances that God was in charge and knew what He was doing resonated with this couple. By giving up control of their lives to God completely, they would find greater satisfaction and peace than any well executed plans of their own could produce. That wisdom was born out of our experiences all those years ago with that young couple going through a similar experience. That desperate, courageous mom all those years ago was now helping our friends in their greatest hour of need. Her story, and the impactful life her daughter has lived, gave inspiration and strength to a couple she will never meet in this lifetime.

___

The decision was made to trust God with this new life, and that little guy has already blessed them more than they could ever imagine. They cannot conceive of a life without him in it. All of us feel privileged to be a part of this new life and marvel at how God can take the worst moments of our lives and use them for the good of many others.

You are blessed to be a blessing. Like the patriarch Abraham, God has destined you to be a help and inspiration to others. Your clinging to God in your darkest days will not only help you to survive the trials you are in, but they will help people in ways you never expected. So be generous with your story, be willing to let others go to school on you. You don't have to have all the answers, you don't have to have any of the answers. You just have to point people to the One who does!

CHAPTER NINE

One Of Those Days

Sometimes it's just one thing after another. You know what I mean. You wake up late; somehow the alarm didn't go off. The kids are cranky, and the toast is burnt. Your wife left the car on empty, and you left your wallet at home. The delays have put you right in the middle of the morning traffic jam, and you're going to be late for that important meeting. You finally resign yourself to having "one of those days." Left to simmer in a pot of frustration, it's hard to see the point. But it's there. You just have to look a little closer. Opportunities abound, because people are watching. They know what you know – anybody can keep a good attitude when everything is going right. But keeping your cool under pressure, that's another story. Under the dark cloud of aggravation and disappointment, all bets are off. If you can find a way, you'll stand out. So, few do. But if your strength shows through, your influence will grow. People will ask what your secret is. See, they have their battles too. They want to know. And you can be ready to help, if you can just find a way to keep yourself in control. So how do you do it? How do you stay on track when everything's coming apart? If part of your purpose is to help others through their dark times, how do you get through your own? Have no fear, help is on the way. Others have walked this path before you, and God made sure their stories were available to you. You can go to school on them, watching what they did right, and learning from their stumbles. The Apostle Paul has taught us before in this dance of life, and he may be of help with these steps as well. Let's look in on him now, during one of the darkest times of his life. You'll find the account in the book of Acts, chapter 27.

Talk about your rough business trip. After being falsely accused-his very life at stake-Paul is shipped off to Rome, to state his case before Caesar. No one listened to him about the lies being told against him, and no one was listening now. See, the ship is going down. He's certain of it. Even though the weather looks fine, even favorable, their vessel had an appointment with Davy Jones' Locker. He warns them, but they're deaf to him. "What does he know, he's just a preacher, and a broken down one at that. He's been accused by his own people, he's nobody. We know what we're doing, and we're sailing on to big profits and into the arms of warm maidens." Sure enough, as soon as they clear the harbor, the winds begin to pick up. Before long, it's howling, and the crew is getting desperate. As the seas rise, so does the fear. Seasoned sailors, who know just how cruel the seas can be, begin to panic. They start throwing stuff overboard, hoping to lighten the ship's load so it can ride out the storm. Nothing works, and despair begins to set in.

Paul's in the same boat as the rest of them, literally, and yet somehow, he's as cool as the other side of the pillow. He calls for their attention, and this time he gets it. "Why isn't he worried," they murmur to one another. "He's in as much trouble as we are." But Paul is confident, because he has had a visit during the night. An angel of the Lord has assured him that they would be shipwrecked, but that they would survive. Paul encourages them to stay calm, to put their trust in God who has not abandoned them, and to prepare themselves for the worst. He invites them to eat something to keep up their strength. Such generosity towards those who've treated him with such disdain! Confidence and generosity–now that's a rare combination. It gets people's attention, and it increases your influence. These weren't attributes Paul possessed on his own. He had plenty of shortcomings. But God's presence in the storm was his strength. Knowing He was there made all the difference. And it will for you too. So be generous with your assurances. Let people know that God will never abandon them, and that He is more than able to overcome any obstacle.

The story doesn't end here. Join me in the crow's nest of the doomed ship as we watch what transpires. Peering through the swirling winds and rain, we see the peril below. The ship has run aground, and is beginning to break up, just as Paul predicted. Fearing an escape, the soldiers onboard rush to kill the prisoners, including Paul. "No good deed goes unpunished," so the saying goes. Paul has kept them together, encouraged them, and this is his reward? Who would have blamed him if he had given in to despair? He's worn out. He's exhausted by the ordeal. He's unappreciated. But help comes from an unexpected source. The centurion in charge of the soldiers vetoes their evil plan. He has seen something in Paul, something noble, something good. No one else stepped up like Paul did. Perhaps it was the centurion's sense of justice that guided him. Or maybe he wanted to speak with Paul about the source of his strength. One thing is certain, without his intervention Paul and the other prisoners would have lost their lives on that tragic vessel. Instead, everyone is ordered to abandon ship and swim for shore. Those who couldn't swim grabbed planks of wood from the wreckage and floated in on the tide. Miraculously, everyone made it, as part of God's purpose became clear.

They'd landed on the island of Malta. A welcoming fire was built for them by the natives, warming them from the cold and rain. Just when it seemed like things were looking up for Paul, a snake slithers out of the woodpile and up his arm, biting him on the hand! Isn't that the way it goes? You finally see some relief, when another challenge comes out of nowhere! But this new challenge would reveal God's heart for people everywhere. The people superstitiously assumed this snake was a sign from heaven, signaling the guilt of Paul. "He escaped the sea, but justice is being served" they thought, as they waited for him to swell up and drop dead from the poison. Instead, Paul simply shook the thing into the fire, and was unharmed. After it became clear he would suffer no ill effects from the snakebite, they switched their opinion. Instead of an obviously guilty prisoner, he was now presumed to be a god. They brought their sick to him, and Paul prayed for them. God touched them, and they were all healed. The worst of times had become an opportunity to see God's power. Without the storm, without the shipwreck, these folks would never have seen how much God loved them.

It's that way for us, too. A fender bender puts us in contact with someone we would otherwise never meet. An opportunity to show the grace of God! Or a terrible health diagnosis puts us in the orbit of a whole new world, doctors, nurses and fellow patients we would rather have never known. But there it is again, a chance to show them who God is.

—

Several years ago, my friend Denise was diagnosed with breast cancer. As she began her treatments, she noticed that many of the patients undergoing chemo did so alone, with no apparent family or friends to be with them as they faced down this terrible disease. She began asking her son to bring smoothies for the others who were receiving care during her sessions. That simple act of generosity made such a difference for those who were suffering alongside her. Before long, she had started a support network for others enduring the difficult ordeal of cancer treatments. Patients could share their fears, and receive encouragement to not give up the fight. Her responses are filled with hope born out of her own experiences of dancing in the dark with her Heavenly Father. Her generous response to her own dark time of life has touched so many lives. Instead of allowing the darkness to rule her, she decided to help others in similar situations. Now fully recovered and healthy, Denise continues to reach out and support others going through the darkest times of their lives. She is a steady reminder that God never wastes painful times, but uses them to position us where we can help others going through similar trials.

So the next time you're short on confidence, remember my friend Denise. If grace and generosity seem to elude you in frustrating circumstances, look around. There are people watching, who desperately need to see the calming presence of God. Don't try to fake it, they'll see right through you. Instead, ask God to meet you where you are. A visit from Him can do wonders for your outlook!

CHAPTER TEN

Left For Dead

From the depths of unconsciousness, he hears himself ask: "Where am I? How did I get here? Why does my head hurt this bad?" Then it all comes rushing back to him – the crowd turning against him, suddenly morphing into a murderous mob. It had all been going so well – people were receiving the good news that Jesus had saved them from their sin. They had been so open, so willing to embrace his message, that he had to convince them not to worship him but the one who had sent him. It had looked like the beginning of a beautiful season, but in a moment everything changed.

Can you relate? Have you ever been on top of the world one moment, and in the next had the bottom fall out on you? Your social media accounts were blowing up, everyone praising your wit and wisdom, but then they were unfriending you in droves? You could do no wrong, and now no one will take your call. You were the golden child, on the fast track to success, but then it all went wrong. Life can do that to you. That's why chasing the idol of popularity is so dangerous. People can be fickle, no doubt about it. Like the old Eagles song "New Kid in Town" says, "they'll never forget you till somebody new comes along…"

Sometimes the darkness is even worse because you once had the spotlight shine on you so brightly. If you are not careful, you'll get stuck looking in the rearview mirror, longing for the good old days when you were on top. But if you drive your life that way, constantly looking backwards, you'll miss what's coming up ahead! Jesus said it this way:

*But Jesus told him, "Anyone who puts a hand to the plow and then looks
back is not fit for the Kingdom of God." (Luke 9:62 NLT)*

Does this mean He's kicking you out of His family? Not at all! He is
simply pointing out to you that He has so much more for you to
experience, so many more opportunities are coming your way, that you
will miss them if you are stuck in the past. He wants to show you how
to keep moving even in the midst of disappointment. And you can't do
that until you give up the senseless pursuit of popularity.

But how do you do that? Doesn't everyone want to be liked? Sure! But
that desire will never be fulfilled until you find full acceptance in Christ
Jesus. Did you know, He's crazy about you? And no matter what you
do, He is never going to change His mind about you. That's because His
opinion of you is not based on your behavior – He decided to love you
before you were ever born! When you know what He says is true about
you, and you accept that He is a better judge of your worth than you are,
you will find peace even in the storms of rejection.

Your worth is not based on what others think about you, or even what
you think about you. Your worth is determined by the price paid for you.

Let me explain. I'm not a big fan of Picasso's work. They say he was a
genius, and they're probably right. I guess I just don't have an ability to
appreciate his art. But those who can have demonstrated how much they
value his pieces by paying huge sums of money to own them. Now, if
you were to give me one of his paintings, would it be wise for me to
throw it out in the garbage just because I don't happen to like it?
Absolutely not! I can guarantee you I would take great care of it,
because of its great monetary value. It would have great worth in my
eyes, even though I don't like the way it looks, because its price has
been set by what others are willing to pay for it. In the same way, I may
not be crazy about my own worth, but the price paid for me was
enormous.

*Don't you realize that your body is the temple of the Holy Spirit, who
lives in you and was given to you by God? You do not belong to yourself,
for God bought you with a high price. (1 Corinthians 6:19-20 NLT)*

What was the price paid for you and me? Nothing less than the blood of Christ, the rarest commodity known to man. There has only been one sinless man in the history of the universe, and His name is Jesus. That makes His blood beyond rare, and the rarer a thing is, the more expensive it is. Personally, I think He overpaid for me, but that is what He thought I was worth, so that price determines my value. The same is true for you. You may not even like yourself right now, but that doesn't change what He thinks you are worth. So don't sell yourself short! Even in your poorest condition, you are worth more than all of the wealth the world has to offer. Knowing that truth can change your perspective as you navigate the challenges others bring into your life.

Let's check back in on our friend Paul. As he came to consciousness, he remembered the whole sordid affair: longtime enemies had come into town and turned the crowd against him by spreading tired old lies about his character. The people who were just proclaiming him a god amongst them now were calling for his death! They picked up the biggest rocks they could carry and stoned him to death. Evidently, they had dragged his lifeless body outside of the city and left him for dead. But here he was, alive and kicking. God must have raised him from the dead, and Paul was not about to waste the opportunity that was presented to him. He stormed back into town and let them see just what his God was capable of. If this had happened today, it would have gone viral in 5 minutes! Imagine the stunned onlookers, the very ones who thought they had stoned him and thrown him out of their lives, now seeing a resurrected Paul preaching God's forgiveness? Talk about staging! Talk about a captive audience! God really knows how to give you a platform-one that cannot be ignored.

Where did Paul find that kind of strength? The answer is found in his statement in 2 Timothy 1:12:

I am suffering now because I tell the Good News, but I am not ashamed, because I know Jesus, the One in whom I have believed. And I am sure he is able to protect what he has trusted me with until that day. (2 Timothy 1:12 NCV)

Paul knew who **Jesus** was, and because of that, He knew who **he** was. Paul was loved on his best day, and he was loved on his worst day. He was loved when he was popular with the people, and he was loved when they rejected him. And the same is true for you! You are loved with an everlasting love, by a God who will never change His mind about you. He loves you when you are being your best version of yourself, and He loves you when you hope no one ever finds out what you just thought or did. And when you know that, you can rise above the greatest disappointments and heartaches life can throw at you!

This knowledge can help us in our relationships with one another. Too often we try to gain status and worth by association. If we can just hang with the right group, we will be well liked. But we can be tempted to shun those who might hurt our standing. Anyone who's ever eaten their lunch alone at school can attest to that truth. Through the years, in my role as a pastor, I have experienced both sides of that coin.

A number of years ago, a man in my church came to me and told me he wanted to be my friend. He was adamant that God had assigned him to be a true friend to me. I thanked him, and told him it would be an honor to be counted in his friendship circle. But I felt impressed to warn him about what he might be getting himself into. "Before you commit yourself to this relationship, let me tell you what is likely to happen for you. As a public figure, I go through seasons of varying opinions about my value amongst those I have the privilege of leading. At that time, I was riding a wave of popularity, with many people singing my praises." I told him that in such times, he would benefit by being known as my friend. People would be impressed that he knew me, personally, and would consider him of more worth because he had access to my "inner circle." But I told him, another season was no doubt coming, when I would be on the other end of the spectrum. In such times, when public opinion turns against me, you will find that being called my friend is a negative–guilt by association. "You will be reviled by those who feel you are either being duped or you are aiding and abetting a terrible criminal!" Often, I related to him, these changes of opinion will have no basis in fact. There would be times when I was receiving way more credit than I deserved, and there would be other times when I was not the fool they were making me out to be. It simply comes with the territory. And if he was going to be my friend, he would be wise to count the cost to him personally of riding the changing tides of public opinion about our value as people. Thankfully he said he was all in, and during our years together, he was a great blessing to me.

Jesus told us the same thing would happen as we followed Him. Look what He says in the book of Matthew:

Students are to be like their teacher, and slaves are to be like their master. And since I, the master of the household, have been called the prince of demons, the members of my household will be called by even worse names! (Matthew 10:25 NLT2)

You are not defined by what people think of you. Their opinion will vary no matter what you do or don't do. But you have value and worth because you are loved by God, on your worst day as well as your best. He treasures you, and paid for you with his son's life. Hold your head up, and know that you are more valuable to Him than all the riches this world could offer.

CHAPTER ELEVEN

The Platform Of Pain

"Stretch out your hand." The command came from Jesus Himself, and it seemed such a cruel thing to ask. "Everyone already knows I'm cursed. Everyone knows I'm not one of God's favorites." Born with this hateful deformed hand, proof of being passed over by God when He was handing out his best gifts, he'd been hiding it all of his life. Tucking it into the folds of his robe so no one would see how out of favor he was with God. Trying to hold onto his hope, but so discouraged at always being on the outside looking in. Others were blessed, but not him. Those who seemed to live in perpetual sunshine, while he lurked in the shadows, trying to blend in but constantly afraid of being unmasked as the fraud he knew himself to be.

And now Jesus is telling him to come out of those shadows, to reveal to everybody the hated weakness that was his wretched hand. Couldn't Jesus have helped him in private, away from so many disapproving eyes? Why make a public spectacle of him, embarrassing and humiliating him in the process?

If you know this story you know how it all turns out–but don't get into too big a hurry to get to the ending. Put yourself in this man's sandals for a minute–he doesn't know why Jesus is making this request. He doesn't yet know that God is going to bring him out of the darkness and into his marvelous light! Look at just the first part of that verse:

He looked around at them in anger and, deeply distressed at their stubborn hearts, said to the man, "Stretch out your hand." (Mark 3:5 NIV)

Now we know, because we've peeked at the ending of this story, that Jesus is going to heal this man. He is going to give him a brand-new hand, one that looks and works normally. But as with all of our blessings from God, He has a bigger plan in mind. He was about to give this man the ability to help others to see the goodness of our God long after he died. He was going to give to this former outsider one of the greatest promises in the Bible–a promise first given to the great patriarch Abraham:

"I will make you into a great nation and I will bless you; I will make your name great, and you will be a blessing. I will bless those who bless you, and whoever curses you I will curse; and all peoples on earth will be blessed through you." (Genesis 12:2-3 NIV)

This promise was not given just to Abraham. The New Testament tells us that as followers of Christ, we've been given all of the promises of Abraham:

You belong to Christ, so you are Abraham's descendants. You will inherit all of God's blessings because of the promise God made to Abraham. (Galatians 3:29 NCV)

The truth is, every time God blesses you, He does it so that people around you will be blessed too! This man with the deformed hand did not see himself as "blessed" before he was healed. But his pain became a platform for God's power and compassion to be revealed! It was a light shining in the darkness, showing people that God was so much more than the religious leaders were presenting to them. He was not an angry God, waiting to catch His children in the act of sin. He was not that impossible-to-please deity that others wanted to use to control their followers. Rather, He was the God of the impossible, the God who heals, the God who is close to the broken hearted, who sees and hears your pain and can do something about it!

Jesus is asking this man to trust Him, to let Him put him on display, to use his pain as a platform, and when he did, was he ever rewarded!

He stretched it out, and his hand was completely restored. (Mark 3:5b NIV)

The people there were astounded, but we've been helped too. All these years later, this man's willingness to follow Jesus' instructions, even when it threatened to cause him more pain, is a great example for us all.

God can use you in the darkness, too. In fact, it is often where He does His best work. So trust Him to use the stuff that makes no sense. Let Him use your mistakes and your weaknesses to help others see a God that wants so much to help them too! The world doesn't need another person hiding their flaws, pretending to have it all together. What they need is what we all need – someone willing to let God use their foibles to show off His compassion and power to change the unchangeable!

That's why the Apostle Paul wrote of a weakness in his own life this way:

Three different times I begged the Lord to take it away. Each time he said, "My grace is all you need. My power works best in weakness." So now I am glad to boast about my weaknesses, so that the power of Christ can work through me. That's why I take pleasure in my weaknesses, and in the insults, hardships, persecutions, and troubles that I suffer for Christ. For when I am weak, then I am strong. (2 Corinthians 12:8-10 NLT)

One of the formative lessons I learned from my pastor was how to be real and transparent with those who are called to serve alongside me. One day, not long after I had joined his staff, he interrupted a staff meeting being led by his associate pastor with this statement: "I need your prayers, right now! I have lost my way. I don't know if my zeal for excellence is God leading me to up our game, or if it is just my own nature demanding too much of all of you. I feel completely at sea in all of this, and I need you to pray. This church needs me to be able to hear clearly from God, and right now I'm not!" He then sat down and waited for us to pray for him. I'm sure my mouth was hanging open, because in all my seventeen years of ministry experience to that point, I had never heard of a senior leader being that open about his personal struggles. Instead of losing respect for him, the exact opposite occurred. I saw it as a sign of strength, and began to earnestly pray that God would not only make clear to our pastor what He wanted, but that He would give me the ability to be so real in my ministry. Another time, a few years later, we were gathered for a pre-service prayer and he told us, "Pray for me–my wife and I have just had the biggest fight of our marriage, and I was completely in the wrong. I've got to bring a message to the people in the next few minutes, and I can't do it like this. I've repented to God, and I am going to repent to my wife as soon as this service is over, but right now I need to preach the Word, so start praying!" These were not isolated incidents with my friend and pastor. He taught me so much about how to lead effectively, but this was one of the most valuable principles he passed on to me–be real, own up to your mistakes, and lead strongly through it all. I thank God for Pastor Burt Smith, and I am sure I am joined by multitudes in that gratitude!

As a young preacher, I loved to tell stories of how God had used me on my best days. It was great to share how God used me on those rare occasions that I got it right. But I almost never talked about the much more frequent times that God used me in spite of myself. Those times when I messed things up so badly and still God's grace would cover me. It took years to understand that often it was my weakest times that God used the most. To this day, I would rather tell my victory stories, but God uses my mistakes far more effectively. People are encouraged to know that they don't have to be perfect all the time, and that God's grace is more than enough to cover my shortcomings and theirs.

I remember one time I was at the gas station in the middle of a rainstorm, under the overhang trying to stay dry while I pumped gas into the tank of my car. I looked up and saw a friend of mine who had run out of gas a few hundred feet from the overhanging cover. I started laughing at him, silently judging him for being so foolish. In my mind I was preparing my teasing quips, "You know that "E" on your fuel gauge doesn't stand for "Enough," don't you? He was getting soaked trying to push his truck to the pumps. After far too long a time, I relented and ran out to help him get the vehicle out of the rain so he could refuel. We had a good laugh about it, and that was it. The next day at church, a woman came up to me and breathlessly told me how proud she was to call me her pastor. She said, "I was stopped at the traffic signal yesterday in the pouring rain, when I looked out my window and saw you so selflessly helping that poor man get his truck to the pumps and out of the downpour. You are such an amazing example of the grace and mercy of our God!" Apparently, she hadn't been there long enough to see my hesitation to help. I thanked her for her compliments, but then told her the rest of the story. The example of grace in the story was not my selfless service, but that God didn't allow me to stay in my selfish, mocking attitude long enough to cause this woman to be embarrassed that I was her pastor! We laughed together, yet I've never forgotten how close I came to having a negative influence not only on my poor needy friend who'd run out of gas, but on this wonderful, gracious woman in my church as well. I came so close to messing up a bunch of people that day, only to have God once again save me from myself!

So don't be afraid to show your weaknesses. Let God use them to be of help to other flawed human beings. We all have our dark days, but God is great at redeeming those times and making us a blessing anyway!

CHAPTER TWELVE

Turning Wounds Into Scars

Slivers were my worst fear growing up. We lived out in the country, with miles of forest stretching out behind our little house. My brothers and I loved roaming those woods, but one danger loomed great there—the dreaded sliver. With all the tree climbing, fort building, and log rolling, it was just a matter of time before some tiny piece of those great firs would end up in your finger. No big deal, you hardly noticed it at the time. But over time, left untended, the tiny invader would cause a pain so acute that you wouldn't let anyone near it!

The problem was, my mom was incredibly diligent in her care for her kids. She would notice me wincing as I hid my wounded hand, and would swoop in for a closer look. She would see the injury and begin warning me of the dangers of leaving the sliver intact. To hear her tell it, blood poisoning was practically guaranteed, red streaks would soon be running up my arm, and left untended, would result in gangrene and amputation. So convinced of the mortal danger I faced, she would immediately run and get her sewing kit, sterilize a needle in the flame of the gas stove, and start digging to China. She would prod and pull until she was sure there was no speck of sliver left to kill me off. All of this was incredibly painful, of course, the memory of which was the motivation to hide the wound in the first place. Ironically, if I had come to her when I first noticed the offending little stick, the whole operation would have been so much easier. Without the beginning of infection, the wound site would be far less sensitive, and the sliver far less entrenched. But did I ever learn? Absolutely not! See a sliver, run for the hills! Don't let mom near it! "Not the needle, mom, anything but the needle!" To this day, if I happen to run one of those deadly little suckers into my finger, my first reaction is to break out in a cold sweat!

But here's the point: You have a great physician who is more than able to heal you from every wound. The earlier you let Him deal with your pain, the less impact it will have later on in your life. We too often try to hide our sin, when the best thing we can do is to bring it to God and let Him heal us from our mistakes. But even in those times where we've let it go so long that we are facing years of negative impact, He is able to heal us completely. There are some wounds that are deeper from the get-go, and in such cases, we are often left with a scar. Just as our physical scars serve as a cautionary tale of past injuries, our emotional and spiritual wounds often leave behind memories of God's healing power in our lives. Those scars can benefit us by reminding of His touch on our lives. Scars really are remarkable, when you think about it. Where once there was a wound that caused only pain, the scarred over area is often much tougher and less sensitive than the original skin.

When my kids were still quite young, we had the opportunity to go to Hawaii as a family. Sitting on the beach, we noticed a bunch of tourists riding the waves with a guide on large outrigger canoes. It looked like a blast, so we joined in on the fun. As we boarded our canoe, I noticed that it was made of wood that had seen better days. The bench we were sitting on was quite rough on the edges, so I scooted my legs out farther to avoid the dreaded slivers that would surely cause me to lose both legs! (Don't judge me, I'm scarred for life!) All was well as we paddled out beyond the waves, and then the guide had us turn for shore, urging us to paddle together, faster and faster to catch the wave coming at us. It was exhilarating, until we felt the power of the wave crash into us from behind. The resulting force slammed my knees against that jagged edge, and opened a gash behind one knee that immediately began to bleed at a rate guaranteed to bring every shark in the area to a feeding frenzy! Gone was the worry of the dreaded splinter, now I had to find a way to staunch the flow of blood while surfing the waves driving us toward the shore, all without freaking out my young kids! Sucking it up, I rode it out as best I could, gratefully arriving at the shore with my leg still attached. I jumped out into the water, allowing the salt water to invade my newly injured knee, which brought a whole new level of enjoyment to our Hawaiian Vacation! The whole thing was fascinating to my then 8-year-old son, and I know he was secretly hoping the sharks would arrive to spice up our adventure.

As the wound healed up, it left a jagged scar that I felt needed a far better story than getting attacked by a wood bench! So, together with my kids, we concocted a story worthy of such a beautiful conversation starter. The nonexistent sharks became main characters in this tale of danger, with the gnarly scar now being the result of a shark bite that nearly took my leg off! Having fought them off with my bare hands, with the help of my courageous kids, we swam to the safety of the Waikiki shore, applauded by all of our fellow beach goers that day, heroes all!

Over the years, the scar has faded, much to my sorrow – it used to be so much fun telling that story to our family and friends, with the sharks getting bigger and more numerous with each new telling. Scars, once healed, can be such fun! Well, that's probably overstating things just a bit. But you get the point.

Whether your scars are physical or emotional, they can serve a great purpose in your life. They can be reminders of the wonderful grace of God, of His miraculous power to put you back together again. Jesus Himself still bears the scars of the crucifixion on His body, a reminder of His victory over death, hell and the grave. Those scars are proof of His love for you and me, and we need only look at them when we feel alone and afraid in the dark. Before long, He'll have us dancing over the very turf that caused us so much pain in the first place. He may just use that scar to set you free from some of the things that used to cause you such pain.

Paul saw his scars that way. When confronting those who were trying to wound him with their words, he said:

From now on, don't let anyone trouble me with these things. For I bear on my body the scars that show I belong to Jesus. (Galatians 6:17 NLT)

He was declaring that those scars had freed him from the opinions of others. No longer living for the approval of his peers, he was now free to live for His Heavenly Healer, the One who had given his life such purpose and meaning. Convinced that God would never waste a painful time in his life, sure that God would use those scars to reach those on the outside looking in. God can do the same thing for you. Let Him deal with those wounds, turning them into scars that tell the world of His handiwork. It almost certainly will be painful, but in the end, His healing touch will transform those wounds into beautiful scars. Those scars will inspire others to trust God's hand on the most broken parts of their lives.

CHAPTER THIRTEEN

Street Cred

Scars serve a further purpose: they give us Street Cred…they position us to be a help to others in a way that we simply could not without those scars. Let me explain. Think about the last hard time you went through, or if you're going through it right now, lock in on that experience. Now think about those well-meaning souls who have tried to encourage you through it. Those who want you to feel better, who tell you to "get over it and move on." They quote scriptures, share articles from their favorite blogs, all in an effort to cheer you up and get you back to being fun to be around again. But if they have not been through what you've been through, they just can't know how hard this all is! They say dumb things that can cut you to the core, stuff like "you can always have another kid," as if that could possibly take away the incredible pain of losing your child! Or, the ever popular, "there are many fish in the sea," as a universal remedy supposedly able to cure you of your broken heart when a long-term relationship ends. None of this helps, because they simply have not known the depths you are swimming in, just trying to get through another day in this seemingly endless ordeal.

But you may have been blessed to have someone encourage you that has truly been through what you are going through. No platitudes, no quick fixes, just a knowing, loving reach to you and an offer to be with you as you process your pain. Just the way they are responding to you tells you they know what they're talking about. These people have great credibility with you because you know they have been where you now are. They can bring scripture to you, even the same familiar ones those well-meaning but clueless ones bring, and they bring life to you that

God intended. There is no replacing life experience, because there are some things you can only learn first-hand. That is a big part of God's plan in allowing the hurts that you experience in this life. He is setting you up, giving you a street cred, allowing you to be there for hurting people in a way that you simply could not be without personal knowledge of their pain.

He comforts us in all our troubles so that we can comfort others. When they are troubled, we will be able to give them the same comfort God has given us. (2 Corinthians 1:4 NLT)

So many people are trying to get through life's most devastating experiences by themselves, not knowing that Jesus has been through everything they've gone through and will be there with them too! They don't know that He can help them when no one else can, they don't know that He is just a prayer away. But they may know you, because God has strategically placed you in their lives. He has allowed you to go through some things, to experience what they're going through right now. He has used all of that to prepare you to help, to give you a credibility that they need in this fight of their lives. Did you know that you are called by God to be salt and light in the world you live in, to help people turn to the only One who can bind up their wounds and heal their hurts?

"You are the salt of the earth. But what good is salt if it has lost its flavor? Can you make it salty again? It will be thrown out and trampled underfoot as worthless. "You are the light of the world—like a city on a hilltop that cannot be hidden. No one lights a lamp and then puts it under a basket. Instead, a lamp is placed on a stand, where it gives light to everyone in the house. In the same way, let your good deeds shine out for all to see, so that everyone will praise your heavenly Father. (Matthew 5:13-16 NLT)

Our pain qualifies us, enabling us to go beyond sympathy, to empathize with them, and to ride it out with them. In the process, we can point them to Jesus, who knows what they are going through more than any of us. God made sure that Jesus experienced everything we would, equipping Him to heal us from all that afflicts us.

So then, since we have a great High Priest who has entered heaven, Jesus the Son of God, let us hold firmly to what we believe. This High Priest of ours understands our weaknesses, for he faced all of the same testings we do, yet he did not sin. So let us come boldly to the throne of our gracious God. There we will receive his mercy, and we will find grace to help us when we need it most. (Hebrews 4:14-16 NLT)

As a young man, I used to think people with back pain were absolute whiners. I was fit and athletic, and assumed all people who had problems with their backs were either reaping what they sowed by not taking care of themselves, or they needed to learn how to buck up and quit complaining. All of that changed remarkably one day while I was working on a landscape job in Newport Beach. Landscaping can be incredibly physically demanding, and that was one of the reasons I enjoyed my job. While others had to pay huge fees to belong to a gym, I got my workouts in everyday on the job and got paid for it to boot! On the day everything changed for me, I was doing a much less demanding type of work, just shoveling debris into a wheelbarrow near the end of the day. As I pivoted with a full shovel of dirt, something I had done literally thousands of times before, it was as if my lower back exploded in pain. I fell to the ground, absolutely incapacitated. Working with a crew of guys who had no driver's licenses, I had to beg them to get me in the truck and take me to the nearest hospital. It took several of the guys to shove me up into the cab, and in the worst pain of my life they somehow found the hospital and deposited me at the emergency room. What followed was years of back trouble, with constant, chronic pain. I had to lay down on the floor backstage between services and long flights were just a torment as sitting for any length of time was next to impossible. I once flew for twenty-four hours to Kenya standing up in the server's galley reading on my iPad because it was too painful to stay seated. I could only sleep for a few hours a night, with the pain waking me up to a whole new day of torture. I begged God to heal me, had countless faith-filled people praying for me, and still the pain persisted.

During that time I met with my doctor and was told, "Don, we've tried everything, and nothing has worked. But your insurance covers physical therapy, so I suggest you go see them. It won't help, but at least it will give you a free massage once a week!" With that, he gave me the films from my MRI and sent me home. It was incredibly discouraging, and I ended up on the floor of our bedroom, curled up in the fetal position, not sure if I could go on. Shortly after that, about 2 a.m., I found myself again on the floor, this time in our kitchen, pouring out my pain to God. I asked Him for the thousandth time to take this pain from me, when suddenly a great peace broke over my soul. Though I had proclaimed it many times before, I told God that even if He never healed me from this pain, I would serve Him with all of my heart. I told Him that I trusted Him to know how to equip me for ministry to hurting people, and I yielded to His perfect plan for my life. Now, I had prayed lots of prayers during this year's long ordeal, but somehow that night I knew in my knower that I meant it. I would love to tell you that in that breakthrough moment all the pain disappeared, but that would be a lie. The pain was as intense as ever in my physical body, but deep within me something had changed. My trust for God went to a deeper level that night, and I am ever grateful for that.

I decided to go to that physical therapy for my "free massage," and, as a new patient, was assigned to a therapist who was fresh out of college. She was incredibly compassionate and professional, asking me to tell her my story. She merely listened as I recounted what my journey had been like, and when I finished with my doctor's proclamation that nothing would help me, she stopped me and said, "Respectfully, your doctor is full of it. He is dead wrong. If you will do exactly what I tell you, I can get you right. It will be slow and painful work, and you will not see relief overnight. But if you will trust me and not give up, I believe we can get you out of pain and back to real living again." My eyes flooded with tears, and I told her, "Doc, I promise you, I will be the most motivated and dedicated patient you have ever seen! You can't believe the hope you've given me – you're the first professional I've seen that has told me there's a chance of finding relief from all of this!" It turned out just as she said. It took months and months and some serious changes in my life, but I have now been pain-free for several years–it still feels like a miracle to me!

Needless to say, my opinion of people with back pain has changed dramatically. Gone are those glib judgments based on ignorance of people's pain. Gone are the easy proclamations of "just get in shape for crying out loud!" In their place is a deep well of empathy that allows me to literally "feel their pain." The whole experience has equipped me to help those who are hurting in ways that were impossible for me before.

I know this: when you turn to Jesus in your darkest times, He relates to you as the One who knows-truly knows-what you are experiencing. He came in human form for just that purpose. He purposely took on a human body like you and I have, with all of its limitations, so that He might feel our pain. He knows what it is to be physically hurting; as He was so tormented on the cross. He knows what rejection feels like, when all of His friends left Him alone in His hour of greatest need there the night He was betrayed. He knows the pain of being misjudged and abused by those who should have been safe but were not. He has the ability to walk you through it, comforting, healing, and just being there, so you don't have to face it alone. He will never give you empty platitudes; His Words will bring comfort that can only come from someone who knows first-hand what you are going through.

And when He does comfort you, that experience sets you up for ministry like nothing else in life can. He's with you right now, and He will never leave you. No matter how broken you may feel, He will put you back together again. You don't need to run any longer. Stop and turn back to Him, open your arms and He will embrace you right where you are. You are deeply loved, and He will use this hard time to make you a great help to others in your future. But for now, just let His presence wash over you. Don't rush it, He has all the time you need to heal.

CHAPTER FOURTEEN

Drowning In Doubt

When I was a kid, everyone seemed to be fascinated by eclipses. We'd make special viewing boxes out of cardboard at school, so we could safely watch the moon covering over the sun. I remember the repeated warnings not to look directly at the eclipse, or we would end up blinded by the phenomena. The whole thing kind of gave me the heebie-jeebies, to be honest. I was worried I wouldn't be able to resist looking up at the sun and would end up sightless for life. But then when the day finally came, it really was memorable. To have it go dark in the middle of the day was as stunning as it was sudden. It got eerily quiet, and nothing seemed the same. Even familiar landmarks seemed different, sinister even. The world seemed a more dangerous place, and the sunlight I took for granted seemed gone for good.

Doubt can be like that eclipse, stealing the light from you and making you wonder if it will ever return. And if you stare at it too long, it can blind you to the truth. The truth that the Son is always there behind the clouds, above the doubt, and bringing you life when it appears He has abandoned you. Doubt will rob you of your joy even on the best of days.

Consider Peter with me for a minute. He's just experienced a spectacular miracle performed by Jesus, when 5,000 men were fed with just one little boy's lunch. Jesus had arranged for Peter to be a part of that miracle, giving him and the other disciples the honor of passing out the baskets of fish and bread. This allowed him a first-class seat to the miraculous provision, as he saw with his own eyes the food being multiplied each time someone took their portion from his hands.

Immediately after this experience, Jesus tells Peter and his buddies to get into a boat and cross over to the other side of the lake while Jesus stayed behind to send the crowds home satisfied.

All in all, a great day, a high point in a life of great experiences following Jesus. But it was late, and as they rowed their way out into the deep water, a sudden storm came up, making the long trip even more difficult. Peter, no stranger to these waters, knew they were in real trouble as the winds increased and the waves rose ever higher. In that kind of weather, in the middle of the night, the darkness seemed to be overwhelming. Doubt about the difficulty of their task morphed into terror when, around three in the morning, they saw what appeared to them to be a ghost walking on the water, coming right at them! Peter was as scared as he had ever been, when He heard Jesus' strong voice call out, "Don't be afraid, it is me, I'm here with you!" (Matt 14:27) Still not convinced, Peter replied, "If it is really you, tell me to come to you, walking on the water." (vs. 28)

We are not told why Peter used this request as proof of Jesus' being with them in their darkest hour, but I have my theories. Peter had been challenged by Jesus time and again to trust Him by doing the illogical, even the impossible, only to see Jesus come through every single time. So, perhaps Peter thought, "Only Jesus would ask me calmly to do yet another impossible thing, and a walk on water in the middle of a horrendous storm in the middle of the night sure fit the bill! So he calls out his request, to which Jesus quickly replied, "Yes, come!" (vs. 29) That was enough proof for our friend Peter, and he jumped out of the boat, and to his delight, he was doing the impossible! Instead of sinking down into those terrible dark depths, he was up there with Jesus, above it all! Things were going swimmingly (sorry), when Peter suddenly became aware of the salt spray in his face, and realizing the absurdity of it all, he looked away from Jesus and saw the raging storm all around him. Immediately he sank beneath the waves, literally drowning in doubt, and he cried out, "Lord, save me!" Jesus did just that, catching Peter up from that dark place and together they walked back to the boat on top of the very waves of doubt that had been drowning him just seconds before!

I have a friend who owns a commercial contracting company in our area. In the middle of the last recession, his company was facing the same challenges his whole industry was. Building had stopped almost completely, and he was faced with the heavy task of managing his company through the most difficult season our economy had seen in decades. One night in the middle of it all, he was awakened with a strong sense of God's voice telling him to get all of the company's funds out of a particular bank they were working with, and was told to do so when the bank opened the next morning for business. This mandate made no sense, as the bank was strong and he had no indicator they were having any problems with liquidity. Feeling strongly that God was leading him, he was at the bank the next morning transferring their funds to another bank in town. Later that day, the news came that the bank he withdrew his funds from had been shut down by FDIC. Had he not obeyed God's seemingly irrational instructions, those funds would have likely been frozen for a period of time when cash flow was vital to his company's survival. Because he pushed past his doubts and fears, and went against the rational and reasonable objections he himself raised, the company not only survived, but was able to thrive during that recessionary period.

One of my earliest life lessons came from dealing with doubt. I loved playing baseball, and got good enough at it to start on my summer league teams. When high school rolled around, I had a good freshman year, and was beginning to dream of making the varsity team and earning me a coveted letterman's jacket-a sure ticket to popularity in that era. The next year, a few of my teammates tried out for varsity, even though it was extremely rare at that time for them to take sophomores onto the team. They were quickly sent down to the JV team, as our coaches preferred to have their better players get playing time rather than riding the bench at the varsity level. I stayed with the JV team, telling myself I'd get my chance the following year. Another productive year at that level followed and it looked like my plan was justified. When my junior year came rolling around, I was filled with doubt about whether I would make the squad. My coaches were encouraging me to try out, but as I looked at the quality of players that would be competing for spots on the team, I was completely intimidated, and took the easy way out. I decided I would wait for another year to try to make the team, a decision I would regret for years afterwards. Unbeknownst to me, the coaches had penciled me in to start on the varsity that year, on a team that had every chance of going deep into the playoffs. They concluded that the reason I didn't try out was because I wanted to spend more time with my girlfriend, since JV practice started a half hour later than varsity and I spent all of that time with her. This really frustrated my coaches, and the problem was further compounded when early in the season the kid that started in my place was injured. That had a negative effect on their season, and they felt my lack of commitment was at least partially to blame. The next year, when I tried out for varsity, they had already decided they were not going to give me what to them was a second chance. I was devastated, and lost out on a chance to fulfill my dream and achieve that elusive popularity I so craved! I wrongly concluded I was not good enough, not brave enough to make my desires come true.

Later, in my second year at college, we took on a roommate who had the most relaxed take on life I had ever seen. He decided on a lark to try out for the college baseball team, and asked me to start playing catch with him. It was clear that I was a much more experienced and proficient player than him, even in those practice sessions. But he tried out anyway and to my surprise, he made the team! It hadn't even occurred to me that I could play college ball, since I'd failed to make the varsity squad in high school. The truth is, if I had just had the courage to try out, I would have no doubt had a place on the team, at least in my young mind. (I am of an age that, the older I get, the better I used to be at things!)

This second disappointing caving to my doubts brought about a very different conviction in me. Right then and there, I decided I would not allow doubts to keep me from at least trying to succeed! I've had plenty of times when I've crashed and burned, but the pain of those failures is nothing like the pain of regret fueled by doubt and hesitation. When I'm right, I don't let doubt keep me from doing what God is asking me to do. When I'm not right, and I let doubt keep me from risking it all, I end up frustrated yet again wondering "What if…." These events are so far in my past that they no longer produce pangs of regret, but the resulting lessons have lived on in me. If I fail now, I want it to be because I gave it my all and that just wasn't good enough, not because I let fear rule me. Someone once said that even the brave experience doubt and fear. Everyone has those twin evils riding shotgun from time to time. The trick is to never let them drive the car!

Doubt is a killer-it can steal your joy and rob your future from you. Doubt can become fear in an instant, or it can slowly evolve over the years. But know this my friend - doubt is a defeated enemy! Jesus killed it on the cross. You no longer have to muddle through with just your own thoughts trying to make sense of things. Jesus is right there with you in those dark times, and if you will tear your eyes away from what is scaring you and look up at Him instead, He will raise you up above it all! He will reverse the curse, turning doubt into great confidence. You will know the reality that Jesus has never failed you yet, and He never will!

CHAPTER FIFTEEN

You've Got Skills

Did you know that fear and faith both require the same skill set? Each requires you to imagine what has not yet happened as if it has already occurred. We touched on this briefly earlier in the book, but I want us to go a little more in-depth here. Think about it: when you are afraid, you are picturing what might happen, convincing yourself that it WILL happen. When you accomplish that, a dark cloud of fear closes in and takes over. You can get lost in that moment, living in fear of things that haven't even happened yet, and likely won't even come to pass!

The good news is, God has already given you the skill you need to combat that fear, even in the darkest of nights. It's called an imagination, the ability to picture things that are not yet occurring as if they already have. All of us have it, from a very young age. It is a great gift when used properly, but can quickly become a curse if we employ it in fear's service. God gave us the gift of imagination to help us deal with the very things that scare us the most. Look at how the writer of Hebrews put it:

Faith is the confidence that what we hope for will actually happen; it gives us assurance about things we cannot see. (Hebrews 11:1 NLT)

In other words, in the darkest of times, we have to learn how to use our imaginations for better ends. Instead of picturing how bad everything will be, we can train our minds to see what He has to say about the situation. This is more than fantasy - it is intentionally aligning our view with God's in dealing with very real dangers facing us. It is choosing to use our imaginations as God intended, to see things from His unlimited perspective, rather than our own obscured view. We just have to learn how to focus our imagination on what is true, what is right, what is honest. Look at how Paul put it in his letter to the Philippians:

Summing it all up, friends, I'd say you'll do best by filling your minds and meditating on things true, noble, reputable, authentic, compelling, gracious—the best, not the worst; the beautiful, not the ugly; things to praise, not things to curse. (Philippians 4:8 MSG)

If we are not intentional about this, we will find ourselves drifting from faith to fear, giving life to doubt and discouragement. Left unchecked, this kind of thinking will steal our hope and kill our resolve. But God has a gift for us, a powerful weapon that can strike down doubt whenever it rises to meet us–the gift of faith.

Faith is not denial–it is not pretending that no problems are facing us. Faith is a decision to use our imaginations properly, seeing life through the lens of God's promise to be with us in the darkest of nights.

The apostle Thomas' experience might be of help here. Remember Thomas? The one who got stuck with one of the worst nicknames of all times–Doubting Thomas. But what did Jesus do for him to help him overcome his fears? He gave him a picture, something he could hold onto when times got rough. He showed him the scars in his hands and side, proof that He had defeated death and could be trusted to defeat every other threat that would come against him.

Thomas, one of the twelve apostles, who was called Didymus, wasn't with them when Jesus came. The other disciples told him, "We've seen the Lord." Thomas told them, "I refuse to believe this unless I see the nail marks in his hands, put my fingers into them, and put my hand into his side." A week later Jesus' disciples were again in the house, and Thomas was with them. Even though the doors were locked, Jesus stood among them and said, "Peace be with you!" Then Jesus said to Thomas, "Put your finger here, and look at my hands. Take your hand, and put it into my side. Stop doubting, and believe." Thomas responded to Jesus, "My Lord and my God!" Jesus said to Thomas, "You believe because you've seen me. Blessed are those who haven't seen me but believe." (John 20:24-29 GW)

Thomas was transformed by seeing Jesus' scars personally. That experience sustained him in the days ahead, and allowed him to transform from doubter to martyr. He was able to face down death itself because he had seen the truth about Jesus. Being able to recall that experience conquered his doubt for all times. Rather than Doubting Thomas, we could call him Trusting Thomas now, all because of a picture given to him. Jesus will do the same for you–he says so in his concluding remarks to Thomas in this passage:

Jesus said to Thomas, "You believe because you've seen me. Blessed are those who haven't seen me but believe." (John 20:29 GW)

You don't live in Thomas' time, so you can't see what he saw. Not to worry, God has given you an illustration that can sustain you as well. You'll find it in the gospel account of the last night Jesus spent with His disciples before His betrayal. Jesus knew what was coming. He was about to be arrested, beaten beyond recognition, and then hung on the cross to die for the sin of all humanity. He knew those images would be difficult to get out of their minds, so He preemptively gave them a stronger picture that they could hold onto in the days, weeks and years to come. You know it better as the last supper or the first communion service:

While they were eating, Jesus took bread, gave thanks and broke it, and gave it to his disciples, saying, "Take and eat; this is my body." Then he took the cup, gave thanks and offered it to them, saying, "Drink from it, all of you. This is my blood of the covenant, which is poured out for many for the forgiveness of sins. (Matthew 26:26-28 NIV)

This was intended to be so much more than mere religious ritual. It was given as a gift to overwrite the deadly power of fear in our lives. Left unchecked, our unfocused imaginations can take us to the dark abyss of discouragement and despair. That's why it is so important to regularly take communion, alone and together with other believers. By rehearsing what these symbols mean, we are able to zero in on the truth: that Jesus defeated death, hell and the grave once and for all. Because of Jesus' great sacrifice for us, there is no weapon formed that shall ever prosper against us. There is no power on earth or in the heavens above that can ever separate us from the love of Christ. There is no greater force in all of the universe than the sacrificial love of Jesus Christ for you and me. As often as we take communion, we do so in remembrance of what Jesus has done for us. This picture is more vivid, more powerful and more lasting than anything fear tries to throw in our faces.

That's why the Bible tells us to regularly reenact this communion time in our gatherings. God knew fear would be constantly assaulting us, painting dark pictures of defeat in our minds. So He tells us to remember the bigger picture, the one of Jesus' body and blood being sacrificed on our behalf. He superimposes this image over our imagined doom and gloom, and in so doing, refocuses on the truth that He promised would set us free. When we see Jesus, all other threats fade into the background.

God has given you the capacity to see in the communion service what Thomas saw in person. The powerful proof that Jesus' love for us is not mere lip service. That He backed up His promise to love us forever by willingly dying in our place on the cross. He, Himself, said that laying down His life was the greatest expression of love that anyone can give:

There is no greater love than to lay down one's life for one's friends. (John 15:13 NLT2)

When you picture His sacrifice, you are putting your imagination to its intended use. In so doing, you experience the same metamorphosis Thomas did. You can overcome doubt's darkest days, replacing it with enduring faith, by seeing with your spirit. This is God's gift to you, the ability to see what has not yet occurred as if it were already in the past.

So go ahead and put that visualization capacity to better use-especially when you are facing challenges that make you afraid. Choose to see God there with you, choose to see His great power to keep you in the midst of life's storms. Don't waste time worrying about what you can or cannot do; instead put your mind to better use, as God intended. Grab a cup and some bread, and take communion with Him right where you are now. Jesus will keep His word to you. He will be with you and show you how to proceed.

CHAPTER SIXTEEN

It's An Inside Job

Ever been on the outside looking in? Wishing you could be in there with the beautiful people, experiencing the things they are, but are left outside wondering what it would be like to be in the "in" crowd?

Things look a lot different when you're on the outside looking in. You can't see what's going on, no matter how much you want to. You're the kid with your nose pressed against the candy store window, wishing you could be in there with all that goodness! But what keeps us out? Often the answer is fear–fear that we won't fit in, fear that we don't belong, fear that others will throw us back out.

The children of Israel experienced this first hand. Former slaves, they had been delivered from centuries of bondage. But generations of slavery had tainted the way they looked at life. They saw danger everywhere, and needed to learn how to see the light when things got really dim. God had delivered them, but now they had to learn how to face the darkness head on. He had promised them a land full of goodness, but it was also full of danger. Enemies had to be confronted and defeated. Strongholds needed to be overcome. If they were ever going to know the reality of God's promised blessing, they had to learn how to face down the darkness. And God was going to help them do just that. He is about to show them that defeating the darkness is an inside job.

Let's look at the account in the book of Exodus:

When the people saw the thunder and lightning and heard the trumpet and saw the mountain in smoke, they trembled with fear. They stayed at a distance and said to Moses, "Speak to us yourself and we will listen. But do not have God speak to us or we will die." Moses said to the people, "Do not be afraid. God has come to test you, so that the fear of God will be with you to keep you from sinning." The people remained at a distance, while Moses approached the thick darkness where God was. (Exodus 20:18-21 NIV)

Don't miss that last phrase: "the thick darkness where God was." God is always there in the darkness, in the midst of it, ready to meet you when you can't see anything else. But as we've been discussing throughout this book, the dark times can be so scary, so disorienting, that it can be hard to see Him there. The natural instinct is to run from the darkness, yet in reality we need to learn to do the exact opposite. We need to learn to run to the God who is always in the thick of things, always on the inside of whatever is trying to blot out His light.

The children of Israel saw only chaos, and they trembled in fear. But among all of the confusion, when all they could see was craziness and threats, God was there. He was ready to meet them, ready to teach them, ready to show them what to do to take down the darkness. They backed off, giving into their fears, and asked Moses to go meet with God instead. But Moses knew what we must know: that God is in the middle of our darkest times, and things will look very different there on the inside with Him than they do on the outside looking in.

When Moses approached the thick darkness where God was, He encountered the God of light who knew what they should do to take down the darkness in the land He was giving them. There on the inside, with God Himself, Moses was given detailed instruction on how they should live. There on the inside, he was told how they could experience all that God had for them, even as they were facing the challenges that life always brings. The light Moses found there on the inside was so intense it left him literally glowing.

When Moses came down from Mount Sinai carrying the two Tablets of

The Testimony, he didn't know that the skin of his face glowed because he had been speaking with GOD. (Exodus 34:29 MSG)

What Moses did, you can do. Instead of allowing fear to keep you following at a distance, you can dive right in, and when you do, you'll meet God there. He is the light of the world, and His light will always shine brightest in the darkness. He's there on the inside, where the heartache is, and He is ready to show Himself to you today. Run **to** Him, not **from** Him, and you'll find Him there in the dark. There you will find rest for your soul and strength to face the trials that are ahead of you.

There is a beautiful picture of God surrounding us in unseen ways, when all we can see is darkness. It is found in the book of 2 Kings:

When the servant of the man of God got up early the next morning and went outside, there were troops, horses, and chariots everywhere. "Oh, sir, what will we do now?" the young man cried to Elisha.
(2 Kings 6:15 NLT2)

This servant of Elisha was giving an accurate report of their situation, as far as he could see. They were surrounded by an overpowering force, literally on the inside of a circle of immense danger. Elisha got up and took a look for himself, and proclaimed: "We're good. There are more for us than these that are arrayed against us:

"Don't be afraid!" Elisha told him. "For there are more on our side than on theirs!" (2 Kings 6:16 NLT2)

I'm sure this servant respected Elisha, but he had to be thinking, "maybe the old man is losing it a bit, maybe his eyesight is going…how can he say we have the advantage of numbers when there are just us two against so many?" But Elisha understood this important truth: the physical world that we can discern with our physical senses is not all there is to this universe. There are unseen forces at work for and against us at all times. Just because things look hopeless to you now, does not mean God has abandoned you. He is always there, and He has forces that are mighty, to the pulling down of strongholds! Look at Elisha's prayer for his friend and servant:

Then Elisha prayed, "O LORD, open his eyes and let him see!" The LORD opened the young man's eyes, and when he looked up, he saw that the hillside around Elisha was filled with horses and chariots of fire. (2 Kings 6:17 NLT2)

Those forces protecting them had been there all along, but they were not visible to the naked eye. Once his eyes were opened, this young man realized why Elisha had been so nonchalant about the threat facing them. Truly, there were more for them than were against them!

This was not a one-time occurrence. The New Testament tells us that there is a spiritual battle taking place in the invisible realm, one that God has prepared us for. We see this truth in the book of Ephesians:

For we are not fighting against flesh-and-blood enemies, but against evil rulers and authorities of the unseen world, against mighty powers in this dark world, and against evil spirits in the heavenly places. (Ephesians 6:12 NLT2)

Whether we like it or not, there is a battle raging all around us. We can't opt out of it, because our enemy does not play fair. We said earlier that if Jesus is going to lead this dance, He would be dancing us right through battlefields. This is what we were referring to. He is always with us in the fight, and He has some very powerful armor for you to don while you follow Him into the fight. Turn the page, and we'll look into how God has given us everything we need to come out victorious in this fight.

CHAPTER SEVENTEEN

Dressed For The Dance
Or Naked And Afraid?

God has an outfit custom made for you for this dance, some pretty awesome threads indeed! This gear is designed specifically for dancing in the dark, and each part of it is critical for your success. You might be familiar with it already, though it has been disguised by another name: The Armor of God; and for good reason. Since you will be dancing through battlefields with Jesus in the lead, you need to be properly dressed for such a dangerous jaunt! The last thing you want to do is to go into a battle naked and afraid! As we said earlier, you don't get to choose whether you will be in the fight, but you DO get to choose what you'll wear to this dance. You can either receive Jesus' gift of armored-plated strength or, you can go into the battle unclothed and unprepared (I don't recommend the latter!) So let's look at this outfit together as we consider the sixth chapter of Ephesians once again:

Put on all of God's armor so that you will be able to stand firm against all strategies of the devil. For we are not fighting against flesh-and-blood enemies, but against evil rulers and authorities of the unseen world, against mighty powers in this dark world, and against evil spirits in the heavenly places. (Ephesians 6:11-12 NLT)

This dancing outfit positively glows in the dark—and when you have it on, all the enemy can see is Jesus from the top of your head to the soles of your feet! I'll explain why I say that in just a moment, but believe me, Jesus is a terrifying sight indeed to your enemy. Jesus has already

---

defeated him at the cross, and there is no question in Satan's mind as to who is the champion–it is Jesus Himself! These two went toe-to-toe on Calvary, and only one of them was left standing. Jesus emerged victorious, the King of Kings and the Lord of Lords. That's why your enemy works so hard to isolate you from Jesus. Separated from your Lord, you can do nothing to stop him–but with Christ leading the dance, you can do all things.

When you have on your dancing outfit, your enemy is blinded by the Light of the World. All of the elements of this outfit allow you to be shielded from the darkness. That's because Jesus is at the center of each part. Let's look at what makes up this remarkable garment, starting with what holds it all together: the belt of truth.

Therefore, put on every piece of God's armor so you will be able to resist the enemy in the time of evil. Then after the battle you will still be standing firm. Stand your ground, putting on the belt of truth and the body armor of God's righteousness. (Ephesians 6:13-14 NLT)

Jesus told us that we would know the truth, and the truth would set us free. *(John 8:32)* That's why He starts with the belt of truth because it is His truth that holds everything else together. That's essential because this dance can get really rough at times! Each time we head into the battlefield, we can know we will not only survive but thrive because He is there dancing with us! Remember, Jesus proclaimed Himself to be the Truth, the Way, and the Life (John 14:6) and when we live in His truth, we are fully protected from anything that comes our way.

That truth will guard our hearts since He has become our righteousness for us. None of us could ever be good enough to balance the scales of our lives. We've all sinned and fallen short; no one can credibly deny that truth. But Jesus died in our place, paid the price for everything we've ever done, and in so doing, makes us righteous before God. So we are free to dance even over our own failures because Jesus has made a way where there was no way. When the darkness threatens to overwhelm us in sorrow and regret, we can simply say to our hearts, "Jesus has loved me with an everlasting love. He has forgiven me and set me free to love with abandon, and that is exactly what I intend to do!"

For shoes, put on the peace that comes from the Good News so that you will be fully prepared. (Ephesians 6:15 NLT)

What a pair of dancing shoes! Peace in the midst of the storm. Peace when it doesn't make sense to have peace. Peace even when everything is falling apart and everyone around us seems to be losing their heads. All of that is possible because Jesus Himself is our peace, as stated earlier in the book of Ephesians:

But now in Christ Jesus you who once were far away have been brought near through the blood of Christ. For he himself is our peace, who has made the two one and has destroyed the barrier, the dividing wall of hostility. (Ephesians 2:13-14 NIV)

That peace has brought us a long way–from the depths of despair to the perfect peace He brings even in the darkest times of life. And it will carry us through whatever is ahead.

In addition to all of these, hold up the shield of faith to stop the fiery arrows of the devil. (Ephesians 6:16 NLT)

This shield is necessary in the dark, because you can't always see what's coming. There are fiery darts coming at you in the heat of the battle that you can't see until they are right on top of you. The enemy tries to overwhelm you with sheer volume, shouting accusations at you left and right. He is named "the accuser of the brothers and sisters" (Rev 12:10) and the "father of lies" (John 8:44) and he uses both of those tactics to bombard you in a blitzkrieg of doubt and despair. He tries to distract you from the truth, that you are deeply loved by God and that He has already won the victory over the enemy on your behalf. Your faith in Jesus shields you from the lies that you are not good enough to warrant God's love. You acknowledge that you are one who has sinned, but that Jesus has paid the price to set you free. Your shield allows you to focus only on Him and what He is saying to you there when you are blinded by circumstances. As He leads you in this dance, He whispers in your ear, "Don't worry, I'm here. I'm in this with you. Together, we'll get through this. Trust me, I'm here and I always will be." Even when you've lost faith in yourself and everyone else in your life, you can hold onto Him because He is holding on to you.

Put on salvation as your helmet... (Ephesians 6:17 NLT)

Topping off this magnificent dancing outfit is your helmet of salvation. When you put on this headgear, you learn to think like He thinks, to process the events of life properly from His perspective. Trials, even the most challenging kind, are brought into scale when seen up against Jesus. Nothing is bigger than Him, and nothing can separate you from Him. This helmet allows you to be in your right mind, to think clearly and to keep your head in the midst of chaos. Without it, you're left with only your own wisdom and experience. I don't know about you, but I need to know what Jesus knows about my current challenges–I simply don't know what to do on my own–but He does.

Years ago, the game of Pictionary was all the rage. If you aren't familiar with it, each player was paired with a partner, each taking turns drawing pictures and the other guessing what phrases the drawings represented. My wife and I were absolute masters at it. Not because either of us possess any artistic ability – quite the contrary. The truth is, most of our drawings looked like a 3-year-old had done them. But time after time, we would guess correctly what the other was putting down in record time. Our secret? We would tell each other before beginning, "remember, think like I think." We're very different from each other, but we started dating when we were 13 years old, so we knew each other pretty well. That knowledge allowed us to know what certain simple pictures meant to each other. For instance, I knew that a rectangle with a little tail on the lower right-hand side indicating the state of Florida represented the United States to Nanette. In addition, I happened to know that stars are about the most beautiful things in the world to her. So if she drew a tailed rectangle with a star over it, I would instantly be able to guess phrases like, "America the beautiful."

In the same way, the better you get to know Jesus as your dancing partner, the more you'll be able to "think like He thinks." The more you dance with Him, the better it will get. If you're new to all of this, the Bible is written down to help you learn how He thinks. In its pages you'll discover what He is capable of, and you'll see what lengths He has gone to in order to have this dance with you. Start with the book of John and you'll begin to see just how amazing He is.

To complete your dancing ensemble, you are encouraged to take up the sword of the Spirit, which is the Word of God. This is the first item that is offensive in nature. All of the other pieces defend you from the attacks coming your way in this invisible war. But this last element will enable you to go on the offensive as you attack the very gates of Hell alongside Jesus your warrior King. Let's return to our passage in Ephesians:

...and take the sword of the Spirit, which is the word of God. (Ephesians 6:17 NLT)

The Word of God is an extremely powerful weapon against the darkness, striking terror in the heart of your enemy and his forces. He knows how Jesus uses this weapon in two different ways. It not only takes down the enemy but it also has the power to separate feelings from facts in our lives. The writer of the book of Hebrews explains:

For the word of God is alive and powerful. It is sharper than the sharpest two-edged sword, cutting between soul and spirit, between joint and marrow. It exposes our innermost thoughts and desires. (Hebrews 4:12 NLT)

Notice that the Word can cut between the soul and the spirit. The soul is the seat of your emotions. When the battle is raging, your feelings can get really jumbled up, alternating between anxiety and confidence minute by minute. You can feel at times like you're all over the map when you are under stress, making you unsure which way is up or down. But your spirit is the part of you that can hear God's voice when He whispers. It can pick out God's voice when there is nothing but confusion and chaos creating so much noise you can't think straight. The Word of God speaks clearest in the dark, because it is so different from every other voice there. And Jesus is that Word in human form, according to the first chapter of the book of John.

So the Word became human and made his home among us. He was full of unfailing love and faithfulness. And we have seen his glory, the glory of the Father's one and only Son. (John 1:14 NLT)

With your helmet on, you'll be able to think straight again. Jesus will guide your thoughts and keep you level-headed. He'll remind you that He is right there with you in the thick of things. You can count on Him to use each skirmish in this war to strengthen your faith and bolster your confidence.

CHAPTER EIGHTEEN

Faith Grows (And Glows) In The Dark

God wants to build your endurance so you can outlast any circumstance that may come your way. He uses the dark times to give you a lasting, unshakeable confidence in His ability to see you through. That kind of faith grows best in the dark. We all come to the end of ourselves in the midst of crisis times. Even the strongest amongst us experience a breaking that tells us that we simply cannot endure another moment of this in our own strength and power. But those breaking times prove to be fertile ground for enduring faith to grow.

Faith grows when you don't know where else to turn to but to God. Faith grows when you can't fix things yourself, and in desperation you look to God. Hard times can become a catalyst for change, motivating you to stop trying to go it alone. That is why the apostle James encourages you to look at the dark times differently. Instead of dreading these trials, or trying to merely hang on until they pass, he tells you to be happy that they have arrived, because they will produce such good things in you:

Dear brothers and sisters, when troubles come your way, consider it an opportunity for great joy. For you know that when your faith is tested, your endurance has a chance to grow. So let it grow, for when your endurance is fully developed, you will be perfect and complete, needing nothing. (James 1:2-4 NLT2)

Crisis times always test the strength of our faith, providing us with feedback about the staying power of our core beliefs. Testing times are always tough times, but they produce rich results for you if you just don't give up. When you enter into such seasons, it can be difficult to hear God's voice. But as has been said before, "the teacher is always silent during the test!" Think back to your school days for a moment. Can you imagine how much more difficult it would be to take a test in class if the teacher began lecturing in a loud voice about material that would be on the next test? If this happened to me, I know that, in my mind at least, I would be shouting at the professor, "Will you please just shut up already?! I'm trying to think here! How about waiting 'till this test is over before you move on to the new stuff?" Jesus is the master teacher, and He knows you need quiet times to process what He is teaching you in this trial, so He often stays silent to give you space to grow in your understanding. But just like your teachers in school, he isn't absent during the test–He is right there, watching over you. And when the test is over, He will help you evaluate what you have learned. He will use that new knowledge to build on what He has already taught you, strengthening you for the next battle coming at you in the future.

During the stay-at-home directive we all have gone through in the COVID-19 pandemic, I found many opportunities for my faith to be tested. I tried to walk an hour every day to keep up my physical fitness and frankly to get out of the house to avoid climbing the walls. We are fortunate to have a large network of well-maintained trails throughout our neighborhood, and I would join the growing throng of people looking for similar escapes from the sheer boredom of lockdown. Most people tried to maintain proper social distancing, but there were always a few who refused to follow the rules. Usually it would be someone on a bike who would fly by like they were slalom racing, weaving in and out of us poor souls trying to stay out of their way. The six-foot minimum was violated blatantly, and I would love to tell you that I handled it with faith-filled joy. The truth is, I would seethe inside! I would find myself fantasizing about all the ways I could knock them off their bikes, maybe with a tree branch or baseball bat, standing triumphantly over them yelling "SIX FEET, SUCKER!" I know, I know, not the best side of me, but trials will do that to you. They may eventually bring out the best in you, but they often bring the flaws to the surface first.

Sometimes we don't even know we had those things in us. We bury them deep, covered with coping mechanisms that work fine until the pressure is on. God lovingly brings those things to the surface in such times so He can replace them with much better gifts. For me, it would look something like this: after allowing myself those moments of foolishness, venting my anger at the insensitivities of those evil bike riders, I would find myself musing, "wow, where did THAT come from? I was all peaceful and calm, enjoying myself, and then went from zero to sixty in no time! What's going on here, Don?" What would follow was a quiet time of reflection, asking God what I was really feeling. Was it really anger, or was it something else? Often, I would feel the Lord's gentle prompting to look beneath the surface, to see that there were fears buried deep within me. Fears that I might be exposed to the virus, and then bring it back home to my loved ones. Irrational thoughts were lurking in the depths of my soul, revealing still bigger issues. Was it really fear of infecting my family, or was it that age-old nemesis of the fear of failure hiding there? That I would once again fall short in my responsibilities as a leader of people so loved by God? Ah, there might be something there, let's stay there for a while Jesus; let's consider what that could mean for me…and in that space of quiet contemplation, things would begin to be revealed that I somehow knew would make a lasting difference for me in the future.

When those testing times come, lean into the Holy Spirit and let Him reveal what you are really feeling in the center of your being. There are things in the dark recesses of your soul that are holding you back, and God wants to rid you of their influence. These times of difficulty are rich with potential; truths that have the power to set you free are found in their depths. In these times, God will show you who you really are, warts and all. He will file off the rough edges, leaving you with a much clearer picture of who He has made you to be. Gone will be the need to protect your image and the desire to impress others. You will be left with a greater confidence in who God is making you to be, and find yourself growing deeper with each passing day.

Jesus was unafraid to be real. He was unconcerned with what people thought of Him. When He was tired, He rested. When He was hungry, He ate. And when He was overwhelmed, He embraced His need for His

Heavenly Father openly before His friends. We see this clearly on the worst night of His life, in the Garden of Gethsemane, on the night He was betrayed by one of His own. Look at how He navigated that incredibly painful experience:

Then Jesus went with them to the olive grove called Gethsemane, and he said, "Sit here while I go over there to pray." He took Peter and Zebedee's two sons, James and John, and he became anguished and distressed. He told them, "My soul is crushed with grief to the point of death. Stay here and keep watch with me." (Matthew 26:36-38 NLT2)

Notice how open He is with His three closest friends. He doesn't minimize or spiritualize what He is feeling. He simply says in essence, "Guys, I'm crushed by all of this, I don't even want to go on with life at this point–Pray with me!" In this raw expression of grief, Jesus is showing us how it is done. Life is hard sometimes, and acknowledging that we have come to the end of ourselves is an indicator of strength, not weakness. Suffering doesn't necessarily signal a lack of faith or that we are out of God's favor. Hard times come to us all, and the best thing to do when we are going through them is to embrace them with an open heart.

Jesus' faith was sorely tested in this darkest hour. He asked God to take this terrible burden from Him, asking if there was any other way to save God's people than this current plan so full of pain and rejection. He asked His disciples to stay with Him, to help Him pray, so He would not give into despair. Even while His friends failed Him, succumbing to their own grief and bewilderment at this horrible turn of events, Jesus' faith was strengthened in the process. He was able to say, "Not my will, but yours be done." The very best thing that can happen to us in times of extreme trials is for us to fully submit to God's will for our lives. In that place of complete surrender, faith can grow so strong that nothing can shake you. That is God's desire for you, for you to be unshakeable. For you to come out of the fire stronger for the experience. And when you do, you will find that your faith begins to glow for others to see.

Ever notice that when metal is put to the fire, it begins to glow? It has no luminescent properties on its own, but once it is plunged into the fire, it shines for all to see. The same thing happens with your faith. When you go through tough times, your faith begins to become visible to others. Anyone can navigate the good times, but when everything is going wrong, your reactions get noticed. People are watching you because God has destined you to be a person of influence. He wants your life to light the way for others to find Him in the dark. Look at what Jesus says about you:

"You are the light of the world—like a city on a hilltop that cannot be hidden. No one lights a lamp and then puts it under a basket. Instead, a lamp is placed on a stand, where it gives light to everyone in the house. In the same way, let your good deeds shine out for all to see, so that everyone will praise your heavenly Father. (Matthew 5:14-16 NLT2)

Years ago, when I was a fairly young pastor, I had a visit from one of my younger brother's childhood friends. He had been a fairly regular visitor to our family's home, especially in his teenage years, but I hadn't seen him for a few years. He told me that he had gone through some particularly trying times, and wondered if we could talk. I was delighted to see him again, and asked him to tell me his story. He told me of the pain he was currently experiencing, and then made an observation that has stuck with me to this day. He said, "you know, Don, your family hasn't always had it easy. Over the years, I've seen you go through plenty of trials and heartaches. But through it all, you have never lost your joy or satisfaction with your lives. You have remained steady through all the ups and downs, and that is so different from what I am experiencing in this most difficult time of my life. I realize I don't have that kind of strength in me, and the only conclusion I can come to is that it must have something to do with your faith in God. So here's my idea: I'd like to read all the main books of religious faith, and see which one makes the most sense. Maybe somewhere in there I will find a foundation that is as rock solid as your family's." I was amazed at his sincerity and his honest appraisal of his own lack of strength in the face of so much pain. I encouraged him to go for it, with this piece of advice. "If I were you, I'd start with the Bible, because it is going to set the standard for all the other works you read. You will see what the truth is, because God has promised you that "if you seek Him, you will find Him, if you seek for Him with all of your heart." *(Deut 4:29)* He took this to heart, and immediately read the Bible from cover to cover, before moving onto the other religious tomes on his list. We would meet from time to time throughout this search, and each time he would tell me how he was getting closer and closer to putting his faith in Jesus. "Nothing compares to the Bible; you were right about that... but I'm still not sure I can accept this all by faith..." I just encouraged Him to "keep on seeking, keep on knocking on the door of heaven, because Jesus promised He would reveal Himself to those who don't give up." Finally the day came when he told me, "you know, I'm about 95% convinced from the evidence I've dug up so far, and I've come to the conclusion that the last 5% can only be accepted by faith. I'm ready to take that step, and put my faith in Jesus." My friend Dennis has never looked back. His faith is stronger today than ever. He has led many other people to search out the truth for themselves, and as a result many have found faith in Jesus as well. I'm proud to be called his friend, and love how God allowed our family's faith to light the way for him in those early years together. We are certainly nothing special in ourselves, but Faith has a way of glowing and showing people the path to God.

This is nothing new, it has been going on as long as Christianity has existed. In the first century A.D. a pandemic plague hit the Roman world, killing up to five thousand people a day. No one knew the cause of the disease, only that it was highly contagious. Fear ruled the day and those who became infected were thrown out into the streets, left to die alone by their family and friends.

The Christian's response to that terrifying time was very different: they tended to the sick and dying at great risk to themselves. Many of them succumbed to the disease themselves, but other believers took their places as they continued to care for those who were infected. They did this not only for their own community, but for the pagans as well. Their selfless acts of courageous care did not go unnoticed by the Roman citizens. They became known throughout the empire, earning a reputation for sacrificial love that would last through the centuries of Roman rule.

They continued to care for the most needy and vulnerable of society regardless of the risk or cost to them personally. In 362 A.D., when the emperor Julian wanted to eradicate Christianity and return Rome to paganism, he urged his pagan priests to match the Christians in their fearless service to the sick and outcast lest them be outshined among the people by the Christian's consistent labors of love.

We have seen many examples of this in our day as well, especially during the COVID-19 Pandemic. Christians around the world have allowed their good deeds to shine by meeting basic needs for the neediest amongst us. It has been incredible to be a part of these selfless efforts, and many have come to faith in Jesus as a result.

When I first came to our church almost twenty years ago, I found a community of people who were reeling. Their long-time pastor had failed morally, and their reputation was in tatters. The church was called East Valley Church back then, but it was mockingly being called "**Lust Valley Church**" by many locals. People were hurting and unsure of what to do. Some were angry and wanted revenge. Others pleaded for grace to rule the day. Having been a member of a church early in my ministry career that went through something similar, I knew there were no easy fixes. But I also knew from experience that God was able to heal their hurts and bring us back together again. And slowly but surely, God did just that. He taught us to forgive. He taught us to have grace. He taught us how to trust again, and He showed us how to laugh again.

As we recovered, we began to ask God how we could serve our community. He led us into one of the most remarkable turnarounds I have ever been a part of. It all started when our facilities director, Jason Beck, took his daughter to softball practice one day. He saw that it had become tradition for the parents to band together and fix up the fields at a local school, because their maintenance budgets were not sufficient to keep the fields in good condition. So apparently, every year at the start of the season, they would spend a weekend working together. Jason was fairly new to our staff, and he approached me the next week and said: "I hope it's ok, Pastor, I volunteered our church to help the parents fix up the fields next week." I agreed wholeheartedly, and so a few of our folks showed up the next Saturday to help, and the parents took notice. As the saying goes, "many hands make the workload light," and the project was finished in record time. Later that day our director was introduced to Principal Bonnie, who was newly appointed to the school. She had heard about this annual parent's workday and was stopping by to thank everyone. Being an outgoing, likable guy with infectious enthusiasm,

Jason began to ask Principal Bonnie if there were any other projects around the school that needed attention. After an initial hesitation when she heard he worked at a church, she began to share that indeed, the school campus was quite rundown and needed a lot of care that they just didn't have the budget for. Jason started taking notes and asked her, "What if I could organize a volunteer day to help with some of this?" There was concern about whether the school district would allow it, concerns about insurance issues and union contracts for the maintenance guys, and on and on. Jason just said, "But if we can work all that out, would it be ok with you?" She agreed, and they began to dream a little about what it would look like. The project began to take on a life of its own, and before long it was decided to do a full-blown makeover on the school campus.

Now the television show "Extreme Makeover" was popular at that time, and it was decided to use their format for the project. "What if we did it like they do, all in one weekend, and surprise the teachers and students? Could we really pull that off? I don't know, but why don't we try?" Marshalling our folks with construction experience, we planned the project, putting the most experienced in roles of leadership that could supervise various crews of volunteers. Weeks were spent in intensive planning; budgets were made and a date was chosen for the project to take place.

Since we were trying to imitate the show, Principal Bonnie agreed to help us make it a surprise to all of the teachers, parents and staff. She told the teachers that there was going to be testing done on the fire suppression system over the weekend so they would not be allowed in their classrooms after the last bell on Friday. This produced some grumbling amongst the staff, but they all agreed to stay away over the weekend. So on the next Friday afternoon, after everyone was gone, we descended on the place with an army of volunteers and heavy equipment, setting up huge lights that would allow us to work through the night, tearing out all of the old landscape, forming new concrete pads and walkways, working around the clock right up to Monday morning. It was an incredible transformation, and somehow the local news stations found out about it and sent out their cameraman to capture footage of this crazy construction project. They led with that footage on their Monday newscast. They teased their audience throughout the day with the tagline "Miracle happens in Orangevale – film at 6 & 11." You can view their report on YouTube by searching for Oakview Extreme Makeover 2005.

On Monday morning, the teachers had been told to assemble at our church campus, which is nearby to their school, under the premise that they were doing a 911 drill, which called for all the staff to assemble off campus. When they arrived that morning, they found two limos waiting for them, stocked with breakfast goodies and with Principal Bonnie standing up through the sunroof welcoming them to join her for the ride over to their school. The teachers still knew nothing of what we had accomplished, so they rode together wondering just what was going on. When they got to the school, they were greeted with some 200 volunteers with long stem roses, signs that said things like "Thanks for loving our kids," and a school bus blocking their view of the transformed school-just like the T.V. show. Principal Bonnie was handed a megaphone and shouted, "Bus driver, MOVE THAT BUS!" with all of the volunteers joining in.

The looks on the teachers' faces were priceless! Jaws dropped, they looked around at what looked like a brand-new campus. Fresh flowers in the flowerbeds, new walkways, even the playfields had been manicured by our people. Parents arrived with their children, TV cameras were everywhere, kids were cheering and running on the new concrete, tears were flowing on many faces. It was an absolute blast to be a part of, and we thought we were all done that morning, but there was more to come.

Later that week, I got a call from Principal Bonnie asking if we could reserve some seats for some of the teachers on Sunday, as they wanted to come and present us with a plaque thanking us for our help. I said, "Sure, we'd be delighted to have you with us! How many seats will you need?" She proceeded to tell me that ALL of the staff wanted to come, and so we gave them an entire section and called it our VIP section, complete with their favorite coffees and snacks. Unbeknownst to them, we had some leftover funds available from the project. We had noticed that their computer lab at the school was populated with the oldest working computers known to mankind, and wondered if we could do something about that. So we contacted the local computer store and they said, "Hey, we saw this on the news. How about we provide all the computers at our cost, and throw in free maintenance and help on top of that?" Generosity is as contagious as COVID-19, and we were able to purchase enough computers to replace all of their equipment.

When Sunday came, we again made a big show of greeting our guests from the school, with more flowers and thank you notes. After their gracious presentation of their thanks, I walked up on stage and said, "Principal Bonnie, we have so enjoyed working with you and helping to make your vision a reality at your school. But you know, we noticed your computer lab was a little outdated…." In came our kids from our children's ministry pushing carts filled with brand new computers, and the tears started flowing once again.

I can honestly tell you it was one of the most amazing weeks of my life. That started us on a new path as a church community. Through the years we have helped many more schools on much larger projects. Many of the churches in our area have done the same. We now are a part of an annual event called the "Big Day of Service" where dozens of our churches and hundreds of volunteers spend that weekend doing similar kinds of projects for schools, assisted care facilities, food banks, and the like. The truth is, enduring faith will always glow in the dark, and when faith meets need, great things happen!

Our church's reputation changed that weekend. No longer "that church where those terrible sinful things were going on," we were now known as "the church that cares about our kids and helps our schools." We had no other motive but to try to help our community, but God causes our faith to shine when we follow His lead. He'll do the same for you when you choose to respond to your own tough times by showing up with an offer to help others in need.

CHAPTER NINETEEN

You're Never Alone

God is determined to build in you a faith that grows and glows in the dark. In the process, He'll put you together with a bunch of fellow travelers on the Pathway of Pain, which is indeed a heavily traveled road. No one chooses this route, but everyone eventually finds themselves along its desolate stretches. There are treasures here, often hidden in plain sight. If you will look around in the midst of your travails, you will find items of great value. One of the great gems you will pick up along this difficult highway is this fact: you were made for community, and you belong with others. Often when you experience heartache and pain it can feel like you are the only one going through this. It seems that no one really understands what you are going through. But the truth is, there are many people who have experienced what you are going through right now, and God will make sure your paths cross at some point. You belong with people who get it, who know through personal experience what you are living through in this moment. That is one of the big reasons why God created the church, so you could experience true community and find strength in each other.

That's plain enough, isn't it? You're no longer wandering exiles. This kingdom of faith is now your home country. You're no longer strangers or outsiders. You belong here, with as much right to the name Christian as anyone. God is building a home. He's using us all—irrespective of how we got here—in what he is building. (Ephesians 2:19 MSG)

As I mentioned earlier, when I first came to our church, the congregation was in a lot of pain. There were many changes that needed to be made to allow us to heal and begin moving forward. God gave me a picture during that time that helped me a great deal to lead the people with patience and compassion. I saw myself in the cab of a large flatbed truck, peering through the windshield at a long and winding road. It stretched on for miles, climbing the nearby foothills into the mountains, towards a destination that was far away. I felt drawn to that place, certain that there we would experience the joy and health that God wanted to bring us all to experience together. I felt like the Lord was telling me that I was looking at the journey ahead, and that every twist and turn of the road represented changes we would have to make to ensure we arrived at our destination. I felt Him telling me, "Don, turn around." Through the rear window of the cab I could see all the people of the church facing forward, standing side by side packed in like sardines on the bed of the truck, eagerly anticipating the journey. It was clear that they wanted to be here with me, and that they were excited about the journey ahead. But we had a problem: there were no staked sides on this vehicle, and the people were standing to the very edge of the truck bed, with nothing to hang on to once we started moving.

I realized that because of my position in the cab, I could take the coming turns much faster than the rest. This was not because I was superior in any way to them, but because I had the advantage of seeing through the windshield allowing me to anticipate when a turn was coming, while they could only see the back of the cab or the back of the person's head in front of them. In addition, I could hold on to the steering wheel for support, and had a seatbelt on that would enable me to speed through the curves with ease. If I were to go too fast, however, it was likely that many of my passengers would be thrown off to the side of the road. They would be left behind unless I took it slow enough that they could all arrive safely at our destination. I heard His voice telling me, "All of these changes are necessary, but you will have to make them slower than you would like. If you don't, many will be left behind. Remember this: everyone that wants to go, gets to go. Travel at a pace that the most vulnerable can handle, and you will all arrive at the destination I have planned for you."

I can't tell you how that simple picture has helped me, especially in those early years when we were navigating so much pain together. God has been faithful, and many have experienced great healing. We have gone through these difficulties together, and that has made all the difference! The Pathway of Pain is so hard that no one should attempt to travel it alone. It has always been God's plan that you travel in groups rather than all by yourself. Look in the ancient book of wisdom with me:

Two people are better off than one, for they can help each other succeed. If one person falls, the other can reach out and help. But someone who falls alone is in real trouble. Likewise, two people lying close together can keep each other warm. But how can one be warm alone? A person standing alone can be attacked and defeated, but two can stand back-to-back and conquer. Three are even better, for a triple-braided cord is not easily broken. (Ecclesiastes 4:9-12 NLT2)

God has people for you to belong to, believe me. His church was formed for this very purpose. As you share your experiences with others, you will find strength and encouragement for the journey ahead.

It has been said that "misery loves company." The idea is that hurting people will find other hurting people, and will spend hours commiserating their terrible lot in life. You've no doubt experienced that yourself. You are hurt by someone of the opposite sex, so you get together with others who have been through that themselves. Before long, you both conclude that everyone belonging to that other gender is not to be trusted, and you have a grand old time rehearsing all the weaknesses of the other sex. You join a support group of like-minded people, which only deepens your conviction that relationships are simply not worth the pain they cause you. As you hear one horror story after another, you decide to never expose yourself to those awful people again. The end result is you end up isolated and no closer to healing from your wounds.

Maybe you get hurt by a person of a different ethnicity, so you conclude everyone of that culture is not to be trusted. Or you have a run-in with people in authority, or with lazy employees, or by people with a different political persuasion than you, and conclude that none of them are worth knowing. As you go down this divisive path of destruction, you will find others who've drawn the same conclusion. They seem to be just like you, just as frustrated and hurt as you are by "those people." It seems you share the same hatred, and you feel like you've found a community to belong to. But beware: what is being offered to you is a counterfeit. It is not the true unity you crave, but rather unified animosity.

Let me explain. Unified animosity brings people together in pseudo community based on sharing a common enemy. We hate a particular person or group and we find affinity with others who hate them too. The problem with this is it develops an "us vs. them" mentality, causing us to focus on division rather than coming together. Such vitriol cannot last because it takes so much energy to hold onto those feelings of hatred. We end up exhausted by our efforts and are no better off for them. Whether the enemy proves too great for us to overcome, or we eventually defeat them, the common bond we shared is severed and we end up drifting away from one another. Or worse yet, we often end up turning on each other as disagreements crop up about the best way to defeat the enemy. We have seen these kinds of groupings form during the COVID-19 pandemic. It seems people are gravitating to the extremes of the spectrum: Open up the country immediately and save the economy, or continue to isolate to keep from spreading the virus to the most vulnerable amongst us. Both sides accuse the other of insensitivity to the tremendous damage this pandemic is afflicting on people. "Don't you care that people I love are dying?" One group shouts, while the other group responds just as passionately, "Don't you care that people are losing their businesses, and those financial pressures are ruining the lives of people that I love?" On each side of the argument is the kind of unified animosity that creates quasi community at best, and cannot last. Rather than helping people deal with their anxiety and stress, they are ramping up those feelings to a fever pitch. The more the debate rages, the more frustrated and hurt people become. But God has a far better solution to all of this. It is called Unity.

Unity differs in that people are brought together not by a shared enemy, but by a common commitment to Jesus as the one who has promised to lead us in the dance of life. When you experience true unity, you will find others willing to share their strengths with you at your times of greatest need. God has made each of us to be unique, with differing strengths and abilities designed to help the others in our communities.

There is a much-loved passage in the Bible that helps illustrate what true unity looks like. It is found in the book of 1 Corinthians:

But our bodies have many parts, and God has put each part just where he wants it. How strange a body would be if it had only one part! Yes, there are many parts, but only one body. The eye can never say to the hand, "I don't need you." The head can't say to the feet, "I don't need you." In fact, some parts of the body that seem weakest and least important are actually the most necessary. (1 Corinthians 12:18-22 NLT2)

All of the parts of our bodies have specialized functions, but none of them can exist for long if they are severed from the whole. The eye is a miracle of design, but it cannot function unless it is connected to the brain that receives its signals and interprets what we are seeing. Hands are marvelously dexterous, but they are lifeless if they are cut off from the body. We are like those body parts–each unique, each needed, but we can only serve our true purpose in community with others. When one part hurts, all the parts share in that experience. If I stub my toe in the middle of the night, my eyelashes feel the pain! And if the tongue gets to experience Ben and Jerry's Coffee Heath Bar Crunch Ice Cream, every other part of my body revels in the pleasure as well!

We can survive without certain body parts, but life is much easier when all the equipment is working properly. It is easy to take some parts for granted. But there are certain organs we cannot do without. They are often hidden and forgotten, but they are so essential that our lives cease without them. They may not be pretty to look at, but we sure appreciate them offering their unique services to our bodies.

When we come together in community, we form a body of believers who are fully committed to each other as we are committed to Jesus as the Lord of the Dance. In so doing, we begin to experience the blessing of community, of belonging. This is wonderful in all the seasons of life, but it is vital in times of great pain and suffering. We need each other's support, and we need each other's acquired wisdom. Remember, God intends for us to become a blessing to all people, and we are given the awesome privilege of paying it forward by comforting others in return for the comfort we've received.

Unity is so important to our health and well-being that Jesus prays for us to experience it at all times. We see His intercession for us in the 17th chapter of the book of John:

20 "I am praying not only for these disciples but also for all who will ever believe in me through their message. I pray that they will all be one, just as you and I are one—as you are in me, Father, and I am in you. And may they be in us so that the world will believe you sent me. (John 17:20-21 NLT2)

Unity is a gift intended to support us and strengthen us in times of testing. Many years ago, when I was a youth pastor in Southern California, we would take the kids on a winter retreat to a place called Camp Sturtevant. This camp was situated in the nearby mountains, and could only be accessed by a five-mile-long trail that started at a remote parking area and climbed steeply up to the site. I was an avid backpacker at the time, so I had plenty of experience in such settings. The same could not be said of the teens in our group. Most of them were city kids and the idea of carrying all of their stuff to camp, including the food we would eat, was daunting to them. I would give them lists of what to bring and what not to bring, which would often be ignored by these newbie campers. It was often hilarious when, in the parking lot of our church we would have everyone turn out their packs that were filled to the brim with contraband items like blow dryers and boom boxes, and eighteen changes of outfits designed for many costume changes during our three-day adventure together. (remember now, this was a long time ago!) There was weeping and gnashing of teeth as I would take all of those items and give them to their parents saying, "sorry guys, but as I told you, there is a limited supply of electricity at the camp, and we need the space in your packs for the food, unless you were planning on fasting for the next three days!"

I would load the stronger kids with the heavier items of food, and put the bread and marshmallows in the packs of those who were smaller or out of shape, without pointing out what I was doing. Everyone's packs were full to overflowing, so everyone was in a position of helping out the group. Finally repacked with the true essentials, we drove to the trailhead and began our collective journey to the top of the mountain.

Since the trail had no branches and ended at the camp, I let the kids move at their own pace, bringing up the rear to make sure no one got left behind. Some of the more athletic kids would run up the trail, leaving the rest of the group in their dust. The less experienced and more physically challenged ones lagged far behind, asking every other minute, "How much farther is it?" I would cheerfully answer each query with "Oh, it's about five more miles to go, and we'll be there in no time!" Mind you, the entire hike was five miles long, but some of them didn't catch on to that fact until we were at the camp.

Every year, the same thing happened. The fittest kids would arrive at the camp at least an hour or more ahead of the rest of the group. With no exceptions, and with no leader to prompt them, they would shuck their packs, take a long drink of water, and head back down the trail to help the kids that were wearing out along the way. With very little teasing, they would grab the packs of those kids and tell them, "the camp is not that far away now, follow me!" They would head back up the trail, sometimes repeating this process more than once until all arrived in triumph at the camp. It was really something to see the selfless service among such young people, and their simple acts of kindness produced an incredible sense of unity amongst the group. Their shared sufferings created a comfort that was not merely for the moment, but lasted for a lifetime. They were living out the instructions found in the book of 2 Corinthians:

Even when we are weighed down with troubles, it is for your comfort and salvation! For when we ourselves are comforted, we will certainly comfort you. Then you can patiently endure the same things we suffer. We are confident that as you share in our sufferings, you will also share in the comfort God gives us. (2 Corinthians 1:6-7 NLT2)

That youth group achieved something significant together. They were willing to share in each other's sufferings, rather than looking only to themselves. As a result, they share a bond that endures to this day. They are parents and some are even grandparents now, but they still recall fondly the experiences they shared in those early days of their lives.

God wants you to experience the joy of unity as well. It is never too late to experience true community. I remember a dear lady named Katie I met early on in my ministry. Her friend introduced her to the Lord when they were both in their 70's, so she was getting a rather late start in experiencing what we've been talking about. She had lived an interesting life that was a little on the wild side early on. That led to some lifelong regrets, which in turn produced some deep sadness and isolation in her later years. When Katie found out that Jesus loved her just as she was, and that He had forgiven her for all the crazy things she had done in her long life, she was overjoyed. In fact, anyone who met her during those days would have described her as just about the happiest person they had ever met. She never missed a church service or activity, treasuring each moment as a part of a loving community. We only had a few years with her before she went on to be with the Lord, but we were so much richer for that season we shared together.

So how do you achieve this kind of unity? By following Jesus' command to love one another as you love yourself. He said if you would love God with all of your heart, soul and mind, and love your neighbor as yourself, you would live a full and satisfying life. It is His intention to give you this gift:

...I came so they can have real and eternal life, more and better life than they ever dreamed of. (John 10:10 MSG)

That more and better life is always found in community. He teaches us to experience that unity by valuing our differences rather than demanding that we all think and act exactly alike. We are not to be clones of one another, rather we are to be unique expressions of His love. If the Creator took the time and trouble to make sure no other human being would have your fingerprints or iris patterns in your eyes, why would He then demand that we all think and act exactly alike?

My wife and I have led several marriage retreats over the years, and we often would include this topic in those teachings. Since we have been married for many years and have been in a relationship since we were young teens, people often ask us the secret of a long relationship. Our answer often surprises people when we reveal that we don't really have that much in common. Our interests are divergent for the most part.

Nanette's idea of a good time is going to a Costco-sized bead store and spending hours imagining all the great things she could put together with such a vast supply of goodies. I tried that one time with her. It was like going to the Laundromat and watching the clothes spinning round and round in the dryers. My obvious impatience lessened the experience for her too. Of course, I can spend hours knocking around Home Depot looking at cool stuff with no plan whatsoever to build anything. She fails to see the value in such pursuits. Go figure. Nanette's tolerance for clutter is far higher than mine. She has a beautiful creative side to her that feels right at home with all kinds of unfinished projects. A few times she has gone to visit family in Ohio during a time I couldn't get away to join her. In her absence, the house is neat and tidy, everything runs like clockwork, and I am bored out of my mind. She makes things so much more fun, so much more interesting. Her life motto is "this has to be more fun," which has probably been born out of a lifetime of living with me!

What we do share matters. We both love Jesus with all of our hearts. And we both love that we are different from each other. I have resolved myself to the fact that I will never figure her out. I don't know why she does half the things she does, but that's a good thing. Life with her will never be boring, and I am eternally grateful for that. With my penchant for routine and order, I would drive myself mad if I had to live apart from her.

Nanette has strong opinions about things, like most of us do. But she feels absolutely no need to convince me to share her opinions. Nor does she feel any pressure at all to adopt mine. When I am pontificating on and on with some brilliantly-stated point of view, she will patiently listen until I've repeated myself a few dozen times, and then just answer me with a quiet "Huh…." It took me years to realize that was her way of saying, "I don't believe a word of what you just said, but good for you for sharing!" It used to irritate me, but now I just marvel at the freedom she enjoys to just be herself while allowing me plenty of room to have a completely different point of view.

So our answer to the question: "what's your secret?" is usually something like: "learn to value your differences." Stop trying to make your significant other into your own image. God made them different on purpose. You already have you, all by yourself. In relationships, we are given the opportunity to enjoy and benefit from the unique gifts of others. The people God brings into your life are different by design.

The same approach will work in all of our relationships, not just marriage. God wants you to be you, just as He designed you to be. You are different from me, and that's a good thing. You will be strong where I am weak, and hopefully I will have some strength that can help you along the way in kind. When new people join our church family, we tell them that we just got better because they are unlike any other person who is already here. Rather than asking them to start conforming to all of us, we try to take the opposite approach. "What do you know that we don't? What do you do well that will allow us to bless others more completely? How can we add to your life?"

The extreme makeovers for schools I referenced earlier are a prime example of this. We once joined with several other churches in our area to remodel a local church building for an elderly congregation. This small congregation of octogenarians were meeting in a historic old building built close to a hundred years ago. Because of its age, it had no restroom facilities in the main building, which is a problem for any congregation, but it was doubly true for these fine elders at their stage of life. They jokingly admonished each other, "Make sure you go before you go to church!" When we heard of the need, we approached several of our sister congregations and asked if they wanted to help. The project had grown in scope from simply installing restrooms to adding a whole new roof, moving beautiful stained-glass windows into the sanctuary where they would be protected from vandals and could be enjoyed by the congregation, replacing all of the outdated lighting fixtures, repainting the interior of the sanctuary, redoing the landscape, and on and on. None of our individual churches had all of the skilled contractors necessary to do a huge makeover of this scale. But one had a roofer, another had a painter, another a plumber, and still another had a window contractor. When we pooled our efforts, we found that we had at least one professional in each trade for each part of the project. Then we each gathered a bunch of unskilled volunteers who could come alongside the pros to get the work done.

It was a tremendous success, and our churches experienced a unity with one another that did not go unnoticed by those outside the church world. All too often the only time the world sees Christians on the public stage, they find us fighting amongst ourselves or protesting against one cause or another. It made a huge impact on our communities and time and again we received their thanks for demonstrating what true unity looks like.

Don't suffer alone. You don't have to live in isolation. Let God give you a community of your own. Ask Him to lead you to a local church where you can love and be loved. You'll find no substitute for the support He will give you through the lives of people who are so differently gifted and able than you. In the process, you'll find that God has given you some gifts that will help the group He chose for you.

May the God who gives endurance and encouragement give you a spirit of unity among yourselves as you follow Christ Jesus, so that with one heart and mouth you may glorify the God and Father of our Lord Jesus Christ. (Romans 15:5-6 NIV)

CHAPTER TWENTY

Dancing In The Rain

Jesus is comfortable in all types of weather. He will lead you in the dance in the most beautiful of times, but He is especially skilled at dancing in the rain. Nothing rattles Him. He knows how to give beauty for ashes, and He has given you a garment of praise to replace the spirit of heaviness when your tears fall like rain. There is a prophetic declaration about Jesus found in the book of Isaiah:

"The Spirit of the Lord GOD is upon Me, Because the LORD has anointed Me To preach good tidings to the poor; He has sent Me to heal the brokenhearted, To proclaim liberty to the captives, And the opening of the prison to those who are bound; To proclaim the acceptable year of the LORD, And the day of vengeance of our God; To comfort all who mourn, To console those who mourn in Zion, To give them beauty for ashes, The oil of joy for mourning, The garment of praise for the spirit of heaviness; That they may be called trees of righteousness, The planting of the LORD, that He may be glorified." And they shall rebuild the old ruins, They shall raise up the former desolations, And they shall repair the ruined cities, The desolations of many generations. (Isaiah 61:1-4 NKJV)

Here God is acknowledging that there would be heartbreaking times for you that can keep you captive, paralyzing you with discouragement. His vow is to send Jesus to encourage you, to heal your deepest hurts and to free you from the prison of grief and regret. He further promises to replace your mourning with joy, and to lift the heavy burdens you carry when you suffer. As He helps you dance in such times, He whispers His promise to rebuild what has been ruined in you, to bring life where now there seems only to be the stench of death. In the midst of the storm, these promises can seem like fantasy, so unrealistic that it makes you feel naïve to dare to hope they might come true.

But it is important to hear His Words before the storm breaks upon you. As we have discussed, it can be hard to hear when you are in the thick of things, so choosing to hear what He has to say to you ahead of time is vitally important. Prophecy has that effect on you. It is intended to prepare and bolster you, giving you a lifeline to hang onto when the tempest rages on all around you. Jesus Himself quoted this scripture and proclaimed that He was the fulfillment of the promise:

The scroll of the prophet Isaiah was handed to him. Unrolling it, he found the place where it is written: "The Spirit of the Lord is on me, because he has anointed me to preach good news to the poor. He has sent me to proclaim freedom for the prisoners and recovery of sight for the blind, to release the oppressed, to proclaim the year of the Lord's favor." Then he rolled up the scroll, gave it back to the attendant and sat down. The eyes of everyone in the synagogue were fastened on him, and he began by saying to them, "Today this scripture is fulfilled in your hearing." (Luke 4:17-21 NIV)

If you are in the storm right now, hear His words and take them to heart. If you are heading into a storm front, may I suggest you hold onto these prophetic promises, that they might be readily available when the winds begin to blow.

There was a time when Jesus' disciples learned firsthand the importance of listening ahead of the storm. The story is recorded in the book of Matthew:

One day Jesus said to his disciples, "Let's cross to the other side of the lake." So they got into a boat and started out. As they sailed across, Jesus settled down for a nap. But soon a fierce storm came down on the lake. The boat was filling with water, and they were in real danger. The disciples went and woke him up, shouting, "Master, Master, we're going to drown!" When Jesus woke up, he rebuked the wind and the raging waves. The storm stopped and all was calm! Then he asked them,

"Where is your faith?" The disciples were terrified and amazed. "Who is this man?" they asked each other. "When he gives a command, even the wind and waves obey him!" (Luke 8:22-25 NLT2)

Notice that verse 22 tells us that Jesus told the boys that they were going to cross to the other side of the lake. As Jesus is sailing along, no doubt tired from a long day of ministering to the crowds, He decides to take a nap. But suddenly, out of nowhere, a fierce storm breaks down upon them, terrifying the disciples. Remember, some of these men were professional fishermen who had spent their entire careers on that very body of water. They knew from firsthand experience how lethal these waters could be. If their assessment was that they were in grave danger, we can safely trust their perspective.

Waking Jesus, they alert Him to their predicament, shouting in panic, "we're all going to die!" Jesus immediately takes charge, and orders the elements to calm down and stop all this nonsense. Amazingly, He is obeyed! The storm ceased as suddenly as it had begun. The crisis is averted, and all is right with the world again. But Jesus takes the opportunity to teach them an important truth that we want to learn here as well. He asks them an important question: "Where is your faith?" I don't believe this was a rebuke of any kind. I believe Jesus was helping them as He wants to help us today.

You see, we all put our faith in something or somebody. It might be in ourselves; it might be in our governmental leaders or our spiritual guides. We might choose to have faith in the goodness of man, in a certain political party or in a particular philosophy of living. But we all put our faith somewhere. Trials test the validity of that placement like nothing else can. Either our faith is well founded, or it is not. If it can sustain you in the toughest times of your life, it is worth keeping. If not, now might be a good time to reassess where your faith is. The question, "How's that working for you?" is not a bad one when the storm is passing by.

Up to this point in the story, the disciples believed in Jesus and had put their faith in Him. They had seen Him do some pretty incredible things, but they did not yet believe He had authority over the very earth itself. They thought He was the most impressive man they had ever met, but they didn't yet see Him as God in human form. They knew the scriptures declared that God was the ruler of the whole earth with power to control the seas. They just didn't see Jesus in that light. The storm changed all of that.

O LORD God Almighty, who is like you? You are mighty, O LORD, and your faithfulness surrounds you. You rule over the surging sea; when its waves mount up, you still them. The heavens are yours, and yours also the earth; you founded the world and all that is in it. (Psalm 89:8,9,11 NIV)

When Jesus asked them the question, "where is your faith?" He was helping them to see that up to now it had been at least partially misplaced. The belief that Jesus was a great man is shared by a great many religions today. But only Christianity acknowledges the deity of Christ, proclaiming that Jesus is one with God Himself. If you believe that Jesus was a great teacher and His teachings are worth following, you will benefit, because His ways really are better than our own. But you need more than an inspiring mentor to get you through the storms of life. You need the Lord of the Universe, the one who has authority and power over it all. You need to know deep in your knower that Jesus is in charge and in control, and that He will never allow anything to harm you permanently. You will experience loss, you will experience pain, and you will endure injustice in this life. But His promise is to use all of that for your good. When your faith is placed securely in Him as the God over all, you will be confident enough to go to your death trusting that He will raise you again to be with Him forever in paradise. Even if you discover the truth of Jesus on your deathbed, your faith will not fail you.

Remember the thief on the cross next to Jesus? He had lived a terrible life, putting his faith in his own ideas and abilities to scam the system. That faith had failed him, and his reward for misplacing his trust was a gruesome death by crucifixion. But in the last hours of his life, he turned to Jesus and acknowledged Him to be King over death itself:

One of the criminals hanging beside him scoffed, "So you're the Messiah, are you? Prove it by saving yourself—and us, too, while you're at it!" But the other criminal protested, "Don't you fear God even when you have been sentenced to die? We deserve to die for our crimes, but this man hasn't done anything wrong." Then he said, "Jesus, remember me when you come into your Kingdom." And Jesus replied, "I assure you, today you will be with me in paradise." (Luke 23:39-43 NLT2)

He no doubt had heard Jesus' teachings during the three years prior to his dying day. The whole nation knew of Jesus' miracles and His outrageous claims of being the Son of God. But until now, he had continued to put his faith elsewhere. Only when he was facing the storm of storms, the one we will all one day face, that of his own death, did he decide to place his trust where it belonged. That decision changed his eternal destination, and that is what God wants to do for you right now.

If you make the decision to relocate the source of your faith, you will experience a growing confidence that come what may, Jesus has got you. That kind of faith stands in the face of death itself, as people have experienced for thousands of years. You might remember the story of three boys with strange names from your Sunday school days. Their names were Shadrach, Meshach, and Abednego. They were slaves who had been taken from their homeland and placed in an elite training school with the aim of making them advisors to their conquering king. These boys were so bright that they inspired the envy of their fellow students. In the course of time, the king issued an edict that everyone must bow down to a great statue of himself he had commissioned as a test of their loyalty to his rule. The penalty for not doing so was immediate death. In effect, he was demanding that all place their faith in him alone for their continued survival.

These boys decided that the God of the Bible was the only one worthy of their trust, and they declared publicly that they could not bow down to this idol of their king. They knew the price for this decision was likely a very public execution, but still they insisted on putting their faith in God alone. The King even gave them a second chance to obey, and their answer to him is inspiring:

Shadrach, Meshach, and Abednego replied, "O Nebuchadnezzar, we do not need to defend ourselves before you. If we are thrown into the blazing furnace, the God whom we serve is able to save us. He will rescue us from your power, Your Majesty. But even if he doesn't, we

Notice how complete their trust in the sovereignty of God was. They declared their strong belief that God was able to rescue them from the fire if He so desired. But they also acknowledged that God would sustain them even if He chose not to intervene on their behalf. If they were killed, they believed God would take them to be with Him in heaven for all of eternity. That belief has been shared by millions of Christians down through the ages. Countless people have died martyr's deaths rather than throw their faith away. That kind of faith is on display in our world even today, as believers living in countries that are hostile to the Christian faith are being killed for not renouncing their faith.

The disciples learned that day on the sea to place their faith in Jesus as Lord, not just as a great man. That faith would be sorely tested in the days ahead of them, but it sustained them to their dying days. According to church history, they all died martyr's deaths, refusing to abandon their faith in Jesus as Lord. They had seen too much to ever go back to believing that Jesus was anything less than God in human form.

Perhaps you have questions now about the source of your faith. Have you been disappointed by a spiritual leader who turned out to be all too human to deserve your faith? Have you felt manipulated by others in authority that have misused your trust for personal gain? I know I have, and it cuts to the core. But can I tell you God will use those brutally painful times to help you get your faith where it belongs – in Jesus as Lord over all others.

Storms can scare you to your core, but when Jesus is with you, your faith will grow and you'll see things you never dreamed you would see. You will discover that He is so much more than you thought. He will be whatever you need Him to be, but it will take an eternity to discover the fullness of Him. My prayer for you is the same as the apostle Paul's in his letter to the church in Ephesus:

CHAPTER TWENTY-ONE

Dancing For A Lifetime

"Give me this mountain! It's mine, and I aim to take it as my own. God promised it to me all those years ago, and I'm ready to take possession of it. I may be 85 years old, but I can do this, because I'm just as strong today as I was 45 years ago! So I say again, give me what belongs to me!"

He was just an old man, past his prime, certainly. So why is he making such an audacious statement about his lasting strength? What's this about being as strong today as he was way back then? Clearly, he's in denial, pining for past glories. Poor guy, it's kind of sad seeing him act like this, one who has been lauded for years as a great man of faith, full of strength and vigor. Why can't he quit living in the past, and accept that life has passed him by? Time waits for no man, so they say. Why does he think he'll be any different?

Surely that's what people thought when that old patriarch, Caleb, made such a bold request of his friend and leader, Joshua. He was a living legend, one of the original leaders sent to spy out the Promised Land all those years ago. While all the others quaked in their sandals, only he and Joshua stood strong in their faith in what God had said about the land He was giving them. But that was then, and this is now. Forty-five years have come and gone, and yet here is Caleb, demanding that the land promised to him then be given to him now. Never mind that this particular plot of land has proven too well defended to take up to this point. Why can't he be content with all the land they'd already conquered? Can't he just give up on this dream, realizing that it's simply too late, that he no longer is capable of fulfilling his desires?

Maybe that's the darkness you're trying to dance through today. All your life you've tried to be a better person, tried to recover the strength of your youth. You've tried to hold onto what God had promised you, but it seems you're running out of time. Life has worn you out, and you're not sure you've still got what it takes to contend for that better life God said you could have. You've made too many mistakes, seen too many harsh things, and you're feeling your faith fade beneath a dark cloud of apathy.

But I want to encourage you today: you can be just as strong as Caleb was, all the days of your life! If you can unearth the source of lasting strength, as he did, you can stay strong to the very end. So come with me, here at the end of our time together, let's go on one last journey of discovery. Let's find out the secret to dancing for a lifetime!

First, let's look at Caleb's statements about his strength. You'll find them in the book of Joshua, chapter 14:

Now the men of Judah approached Joshua at Gilgal, and Caleb son of Jephunneh the Kenizzite said to him, "You know what the LORD said to Moses the man of God at Kadesh Barnea about you and me. I was forty years old when Moses the servant of the LORD sent me from Kadesh Barnea to explore the land. And I brought him back a report according to my convictions, but my brothers who went up with me made the hearts of the people melt with fear. <u>I, however, followed the LORD my God wholeheartedly.</u> So on that day Moses swore to me, 'The land on which your feet have walked will be your inheritance and that of your children forever, <u>because you have followed the LORD my God wholeheartedly.</u>' (emphasis mine) (Joshua 14:6-9 NIV)

Caleb, as he recollected that experience all those years ago, emphasized that he was able to believe God because he had followed the Lord his God wholeheartedly. He had the same weaknesses all the other men had, but the one thing he got right was to follow God with all he had every day of his life. I'm sure some days were better than others, but his secret was this: he gave God his best, every day. When he did that, his reward was lasting strength. He knew what we must know:

But if from there you seek the LORD your God, you will find him if you look for him with all your heart and with all your soul. (Deuteronomy 4:29 NIV)

This scripture was given to the people as instruction for those times when they would find themselves overrun by enemies, taken into captivity by their mistakes and the sins of others. The promise is lasting for us all: If you seek Him, you will find Him, if you look for him with all you've got. Now, my best may not measure up to your best, or even to my previous best efforts, but happily, it doesn't have to! All I have to do is to give God my best today, and I will find Him. That's important, because when we find Him, we receive what He has to offer us. And one of the best gifts He promises us is His lasting strength:

GOD is my strength, GOD is my song, and, yes! GOD is my salvation. This is the kind of God I have and I'm telling the world! This is the God of my father— I'm spreading the news far and wide! (Exodus 15:2 MSG)

That's just what Caleb was doing–he was declaring to the whole world that because He had been wholehearted in his search for God, he had indeed found him. And when he found God, he found the source of his strength. That strength was not dependent on Caleb's youth and vigor, so it could not be diluted by the passage of time. Even in his prime, forty-five years previous, his strength had never been in his own prowess. At that time, he was nothing but a former slave. He had not yet been tested in battle, and had not yet learned to fight. But he had seen God's mighty hand of deliverance, when he and all his people were rescued from Pharaoh and the mightiest fighting force on the planet. His strength began there, when he realized that God would never leave them or forsake them. Through four long decades, wandering in the desert, God had never abandoned them. God was the true source of strength, and Caleb kept Him close all the days of his life. THAT'S why he could declare:

"Now then, just as the LORD promised, he has kept me alive for forty-five years since the time he said this to Moses, while Israel moved about

in the desert. So here I am today, eighty-five years old! I am still as strong today as the day Moses sent me out; I'm just as vigorous to go out to battle now as I was then. Now give me this hill country that the LORD promised me that day. You yourself heard then that the Anakites were there and their cities were large and fortified, but, the LORD helping me, I will drive them out just as he said." (Joshua 14:10-12 NIV)

Look there in verse 11: "I am still as strong today as the day Moses sent me out; I'm just as vigorous to go out to battle as I was then…" This statement is accurate, even though he is now an old man. Because his source of strength in his prime was the same source as in his old age: God Himself was Caleb's strength, and God was with him still, just as he promised. That's why he could declare, in verse 12: "…the Lord helping me, I will drive them out just as he said."

Caleb's example has always spoken to me personally, but with each passing year it has become more and more valuable. It's likely I'm well into the final third of my life, and as I age, I find myself more determined than ever to make the most of the time I have left. It is encouraging to know that I can remain strong to the very end, because my strength is not founded in the physical world. God has been incredibly faithful to me, and I know He will be there for you as well.

Like Caleb, you're stronger than you know. It's not how much weight you can lift in the gym that determines your power–it is how hard you go after God that will make you big and strong! Remember, He has promised to dance you through every battlefield you will ever encounter. Once you let Him lead this dance, you will never be alone again. His strength will be there for you when you need it. When you think you can't stand one more moment of this, He will be there, filling your cup to overflowing. You can count on it.

So, will you let Him lead you? He's there with you right now, asking: "May I have this dance?" If you receive His invitation to dance for a lifetime, you're in for quite a ride–so buckle up and keep on dancing my friend!

A FINAL WORD

If you made the decision to let Jesus lead you, congratulations! I encourage you to pray a simple prayer, like this one:

"Lord Jesus, lead me in this dance of life. I need you in the dark times, and I accept your invitation to be with me in every season of my life. I will follow you wherever you choose to lead me, unconditionally!"

I'd love to hear from you! I hope you'll drop me a line, telling me how the dance is going so far.

You can contact me at **info@donroberts.org**.

Together,
Don

Special thanks to:

*Jourdain and Josiah - the two best kids anyone could ask for –
I love you with all of my heart (and I like you a lot too)!*

Liam and Ellie - Papa loves you SOOOOOO much!

*Joel and Amy - thank you for loving our kids so well, Mom and I
are proud to call you family.*

Pastor Joe - for your lifelong friendship.

Corey - for your tireless efforts in getting my books to press.

*The people of the Life Center - it is such an honor to be doing life
with all of you!*